A PRIMER OF OLD TESTAMENT ARCHAEOLOGY

BY

H. J. FRANKEN

AND

C. A. FRANKEN-BATTERSHILL

LEIDEN

E. J. BRILL

1963

PRINTED IN THE NETHERLANDS

INDEX

LIST OF FIGURES

page

LIST OF PLATES

ACKNOWLEDGEMENTS

For permission to reproduce illustrations thanks are due to the Palestine Exploration Fund, London; the American School of Oriental Research, New Haven; the British School of Archaeology in Egypt, London; the Oxford University Press, London; the Magnes Press, Jerusalem; the University Museum, Pennsylvania; the Oriental Institute of the University of Chicago; Marshall, Morgan & Scott, London; Phoenix House, London; E. Benn, London; and Père R. de Vaux O.P.

LIST OF ABBREVIATIONS

A.A.A.	*Annals of Archaeology and Anthropology*, Liverpool
A.A.S.O.R.	*Annual of the American Schools of Oriental Research*, New Haven
A.D.A.J.	*Annual of the Department of Antiquities of Jordan*, Amman
Albright, *Archaeology*	Albright, W. F.: *The Archaeology of Palestine*, Pelican Books
ʿ*Atiqot*	*Journal of the Israel Department of Antiquities*, Jerusalem
Barrois, *Manuel*	Barrois, A. G.: *Manuel d'Archéologie Biblique*, Paris, I, 1939, II, 1953
B.A.S.O.R.	*Bulletin of the American Schools of Oriental Research*, New Haven
B.B.S.A.J.	*Bulletin of the British School of Archaeology in Jerusalem*
Eggers	Eggers, H. J.: *Einführung in die Vorgeschichte*, München, 1959
Expedition	*Excavation, the Bulletin of the University Museum of the University of Pennsylvania*, Philadelphia
Harvard Expedition	Reisner, G. A., Fisher, C. S., Lyon, D. G.: *Harvard Excavations at Samaria*, Cambridge, Mass., 1924
Hazor I, II	Yadin, Y., Aharoni, Y., Amiran, R., Dothan, T., Dunayevsky, I., Perrot, J.: *Hazor* I, Jerusalem 1958, II, 1961
I.E.J.	*Israel Exploration Journal*, Jerusalem
I.L.N.	*Illustrated London News*
J.B.L.	*Journal of Biblical Literature*
Kenyon, *Archaeology*	Kenyon, K. M.: *Archaeology in the Holy Land*, London, 1960
Kenyon, *Jericho*	Kenyon, K. M.: *Digging up Jericho*, London, 1957
Kenyon, *Jericho* I	Kenyon, K. M.: *Excavations at Jericho*, I, London, 1960
Lachish II-IV	Tufnell, O.: *Lachish* II, London, 1940; III, 1953; IV, 1958
O.I.P.	*Oriental Institute Publications*, Chicago
P.E.Q.	*Palestine Exploration Quarterly*, London
Q.D.A.P.	*The Quarterly of the Department of Antiquities in Palestine*, Jerusalem
R.B.	*Revue Biblique*, Paris
Rowley	Rowley, H. H.: *From Joseph to Joshua*, London, 1950
S.S. I-III	Crowfoot, J. W., Crowfoot, G. M., Kenyon K. M., Sukenik, E. L.: *Samaria-Sebaste* I, London, 1942, II, 1938; III, 1957
V.T.	*Vetus Testamentum*, Leiden
Wheeler	Wheeler, R. E. M.: *Archaeology from the Earth*, Oxford, 1954
Wright	Wright, E. G.: *The Pottery of Palestine from the Earliest Times to the end of the Early Bronze Age*, New Haven, 1937
Z.A.W.	*Zeitschrift für die Alttestamentliche Wissenschaft*, Berlin
Z.D.P.V.	*Zeitschrift des Deutschen Palästina-Vereins*, Leipzig

PREFACE

BY

P. A. H. DE BOER

Old Testament scholars can no longer confine themselves to the literary and historical aspects of the Bible. In former days 'antiquities', taken as a description of customs and objects from Biblical times, amplified with comparable material borrowed from non-Biblical sources, served for an introduction to and the stage setting of the exegesis of the Biblical text. To-day this whole field has been enlarged and at the same time been subjected to many corrections owing to the rise of Biblical archaeology.

This Primer of Old Testament archaeology is no source of information about "the latest results" of excavations in Palestine but a guide to find our way in the often confusing and even bewildering mass of archaeological, semi- and quasi-archaeological books and articles boldly inviting our attention. As Old Testament scholars we may be completely convinced of the necessity of acknowledging aechaeological facts in our research; our difficulty is that we did not learn to read the reports critically, and we remain dependant on conclusions which we cannot control, to say nothing of the second-hand conclusions reproduced in easily read books with fine illustrations. This makes us uneasy, not because of differences in interpretation, nor because of a possible necessity of reconsidering and revising opinions held without sufficient knowledge of archaeological results—(is it not characteristic of scientific work to acknowledge the tentative value of our conclusions?)—we are uneasy because we are unable to check the arguments used in archaeological reports and books. Authors do not always help us, inspite of their illustrations. And so far archaeologists have not succeeded in fixing a definite terminology. This Primer shows us that Biblical archaeologists need to reflect both on their methods of excavation and the publishing of their results.

This Primer is intended for theological students. It's aim is to teach us to read—that first and last step of all learning—in order to get an insight into real facts, distinguishing fact from hypothesis. This gained, the Old Testament student regains his self confidence and at the same time the door opens for collaboration between archaeology and exegesis. Both branches of the same discipline belong together and their going hand in hand promises to be a success if each of them respects the law of scientific research: openness for verification.

PREFACE

BY

K. M. KENYON

Archaeology does not claim to be a discipline on its own. It is rather, to-day, a very highly specialised method of supplementing history in the very broadest sense. This widening of the term history concerns the periods for which there are none of the written records upon which history in the broadest sense depends, for which archaeology in effect writes the history; in a more exactly supplementary sense, archaeology provides a background for history in dealing with those periods for which some written records are available. Dr. and Mrs. Franken have in this book done very useful work in showing to theologians the use that can be made of archaeology as an adjunct to the history of Palestine in the time of the Old Testament.

Their method is both cautionary and illustrative, cautionary in showing that, since scientific archaeology is a comparatively recent development, many of the older excavation reports require careful editing and interpretation, illustrative in taking certain aspects of the more recent archaeological results to illuminate the background of the Old Testament story. It is a book that all theologians should read.

INTRODUCTION

In the last two decades there have been a number of books written about Biblical archaeology and its related studies for the layman. They have nearly all dealt with the end products of archaeological research, the actual finds themselves, such as buildings, coins or figurines and used them to illustrate the Biblical text, but hardly any of them have been written by accredited field archaeologists. From an archaeological point of view this selection is often quite arbitrary, and thus two objections can be raised against the use of such books for the study of Biblical archaeology. First, the reader is entirely dependent on the second hand interpretation of finds and archaeological situations as given by the authors and remains unable to study the reports independently. Secondly, from the selected archaeological evidence in these books it is impossible to assess what the real contribution of archaeology is to our knowledge of Biblical times. There are, of course, honourable exceptions to this misleading way of handling archaeological evidence, but it can do untold damage to the intelligent use of archaeological research for increasing our knowledge of Biblical times and modes.

No book, as far as the authors know, has yet appeared in which, so to speak, the grammar and syntax of Biblical archaeology are handled. This book is written mainly for theological students, and aims to put in their hands the tools for extracting relevant material from excavation reports which has direct bearing on their work of understanding and re-interpreting the Bible in the 20th century. The authors' aim is to provide the theological student with a critical apparatus with which to sort the sensational claim from the sound observation and the following points should be kept in mind when working with this book:

1. The archaeology of ancient Israel is but a small part of the far greater study of Palestinian archaeology, which consists of the excavation and recovery of the cultures of many millennia in Palestine.

2. Two considerable changes have taken place in Palestinian archaeology since the end of the Second World War. The first is that gradually excavations are being carried out more and more by trained archaeologists, whose active consciences drive them on to

publish their finds adequately, in place of no less conscientious but
amateur archaeologists of former days, who more often than not
were professional epigraphists or theologians. These early excavators,
following their predecessors in Classical lands, placed their trust in
architects not archaeologists. The second change is consequent to
this: the improvement in field work and techniques. It is true to say
that now at last Palestinian archaeology is on a scientific footing.

3. It must however be stressed here that this book is not intended
as a manual of field archaeology. Just as various Introductions to
the Old Testament aim at bringing students to the literary sources
of the Bible, so this introduction will attempt to bring the student
in contact with the sources of archaeological claims and counter
claims.

4. It must be remembered that archaeology itself is not a branch
of Biblical studies but an independent discipline. Like all subjects,
it has its limitations. As Sir Mortimer Wheeler has expressed it:
'The archaeologist may find the tub but altogether miss Diogenes'.

5. Apart from the limitations of archaeology itself, nobody can
fully understand archaeological fieldwork (and the published results,
for that matter) without a proper training in field archaeology at home
and some experience in the field in Palestine. This book is not written
to make theological students archaeologists. Only where it is strictly
necessary in order that the student can make independant use of
the archaeological publications, will this Primer deal with intricacies
of archaeological fieldwork.

How important is the study of archaeology for the theological
student or ordinand? As any lecturer in a theological faculty knows,
the student's programme is already filled to capacity with essential
subjects. Can Biblical archaeology remain an optional extra or is it
of first class importance to a balanced theological training? The
authors believe that it ought to be included in every theologians
timetable for several reasons. One of the most important of these
has been brought about by the revolution in Biblical archaeology
referred to above, in which the actual digging of Biblical sites is now,
more and more, in the capable hands of professional archaeologists,
who however in all probability have no particular training in Old
or New Testament subjects. While entirely applauding this change
over, one cannot fail to see another danger looming up: namely
that the textual study of the Bible, and that of the archaeological

evidence will grow wider and wider apart. This would be a tragedy, for both pursuits are complementary to each other—indeed, the authors would go so far as to say absolutely dependent one on another. Really factual evidence from the soil of Palestine must be interpreted not only in the light of Near Eastern history, but also dealt with by specialists in comparative religion, etc. Both O.T. studies and archaeology are such highly specialized subjects now that few can hope to combine both disciplines, and keep in the first rank of scholarship. It is important therefore that some O.T. men will join the ranks of professional archaeologists, but even more so that those who remain based on O.T. studies will keep in touch with archaeology; able to understand its methods and terminology, and prepared to use its evidence in conjunction with their own studies.

It is to be expected that archaeology will in the future provide more evidence for the understanding of the world of the Bible and throw light on yet unsolved historical problems. Hence students ought be able to study the actual excavation reports and not only the conclusions reached.

In short, since the study of the Bible makes use af all sources available in the training of theologians, archaeology can no longer be considered as just a visual aid for the parish, let alone as the last pillar on which the truth of the Bible rests.

Therefore, this book mainly refers to excavation reports [1]). The chapter on archaeological method is essential for the whole purpose of this introduction. Since, as will be shown, the dating of archaeological finds is one of the main problems of the excavator, much attention is given to the pottery of the Iron Age. The number of subjects dealt with in this book is limited. Instead of giving résumés of all that has been excavated, this book teaches first of all methods of study, giving the student an idea of what is found in the soil and how it is found. The following books are recommended for continual reference. For résumés of the results of earlier archaeological research:

A. G. Barrois, *Manuel d'Archaéologie Biblique*, Paris, I, 1939; II, 1953;

---

[1]) The subjects, dealt with in this book, have expressly been taken from excavation reports, not from preliminary reports nor from articles, in order to bring students in as close a contact with the sources as possible. Once the student is used to studying excavation reports, he will readily find his way in the periodicals.

C. Watzinger, *Denkmäler Palestinas*, Leipzig, I, 1933; II, 1935. But both these books contain outdated material and should be used cautiously and critically.

For a good sound up-to-date book dealing with the cultural periods in a more technical manner:

K. M. Kenyon, *Archaeology in the Holy Land*, London, 1960.

For an excellent study of the social and religious structure of this period:

R. de Vaux, O. P., *Les Institutions de l'Ancien Testament*, Paris, I, 1958; II, 1960.

For basic archaeological principles:

R. E. M. Wheeler, *Archaeology from the Earth*, Oxford, 1954.

H. J. Eggers, *Einführung in die Vorgeschichte*, München, 1959.

CHAPTER ONE

A RÉSUMÉ OF THE DEVELOPMENT OF ARCHAEOLOGICAL METHOD IN PALESTINE

Archaeologically speaking, Palestine has suffered from her unique position in the sphere of world religions. Instead of being treated as a practical aid to history, helping to push back the frontiers of pre-history, archaeology in Palestine has in the past—and in some in-stances even now—been used to shore up an interpretation of the authority of the Old Testament. This attitude was by no means always the fault of the excavator. Archaeology is a costly business, and its patrons have often had some religious axe to grind, or some pet theory to prove. This point can be illustrated from the Parker Expedition before the First World War, who wished to be guided in their researches by a crystal ball, to Mr. J. Allegro's treasure hunt for the gold of the Dead Sea Scrolls in 1960. Executors of such pursuits pay little attention to 'irrelevant' archaeological evidence and their publications have often little value.

Unless a great deal of space is used, a certain amount of generaliza-tion must be permitted when making a resumé of methods used. In this way the different methods of excavating and their development can be roughly divided into four different groups:

the Tunnelers of the last half of the 19th century;

the Sequence Daters exemplified by Petrie;

the Architect-Archaeologists of some French, German and English excavations,

and the Stratigraphical Excavators.

Throughout the generalized description of these groups it must be bourne in mind that while some methods developed out of others, entirely superceding them, other methods were merely refined and are still in use although obsolete by archaeological standards in present day Europe and England.

THE TUNNELERS

In 1865 *the Palestine Exploration Fund* was established and Charles Warren, a young British ordnance officer was sent out by the Fund to excavate in Jerusalem. He had to face very strong religious prejudices in his work from the Turkish authorities, and the Jewish, Christian and Islamic inhabitants of the Holy City. So instead of laying bare horizontal stretches of ground, he tunnelled down the side of walls. This dangerous type of digging apparently attracted less attention and was in fact even carried out at night. Warren was working without one single reliable dating criteria. At that time even masonry of so modern a period as that of the Crusaders presented dating problems and the age of different types of pottery was still anybody's guess. So it is not at all surprising that much of Warren's work is uncertain or wrongly dated. The great advantage of his work is that his training as an engineer and surveyor led him to make careful records and notes of what he saw, so that much of what he did can be checked and re-dated now.

At the same time that Warren was working, de Saulcy cleared the so-called *Tombeux des Rois* in the Jerusalem area. These were simply cleared in the way that a sewer might be cleaned out to day. The earth was removed and the structure of the rock cut tombs revealed.

All the other men of this date, Robinson the American, Clermont-Ganneau the Frenchman, and Condor and Kitchener from England (Pl. I) were explorers and surveyors, although they excavated, not archaeologists. Their great contribution was mapping the land with its ruins and historical sites and identifying Biblical sites, and on occasion preserving surface finds.

THE SEQUENCE DATERS

In 1890 Flinders Petrie began his epoch making work at Tell el-Hesi, a mound in SW Palestine. He was then 37 and was to spend the rest of his life, until 1942, working and influencing Palestinian archaeological methods for better or worse. Petrie's genius lay in the discovery of the, retrospectively, simple fact that a Near Eastern mound is an accumulation of one ruined city overlying another; and that each period had its own typical pottery differing from that found above or below it, and that what lay at the bottom of the mound must of necessity be older in date than that which lay near the top. This was a revolutionary discovery. Although Schlieman in 1870 had recognised the fact that there were accumulated layers of deposit at Troy, archaeologists in Palestine did not follow up this clue. Schlieman himself failed to see that the pottery found in the different occupation levels could be used for dating the levels. Petrie's choice of site was a particularly lucky one because a wadi running nearby had, through the ages, carved out a portion of the ancient mound, thus exposing a vertical section through the accumulated levels (Pl. II). This vertical cut stimulated Petrie into collecting the pottery from each obvious level. Another happy fact was that Tell el-Hesi is on the main coastal route not far distant from the Egyptian border. This meant that Egyptian exports were found in plenty at the site, and thus made it possible for the Englishman to ascertain the first absolute dates in Palestinian archaeology. These Egyptian objects were dateable because the rich inscriptional material of Egyptian tombs and temples made it possible to date their associated objects.

A beginning was now made for the archaeological chronology of Palestine. Bliss, an American, and Macalister, an Irishman, excavated four mounds in the Shephelah, and produced a time sequence of four periods: Early Pre-Israelite, Late Pre-Israelite, Jewish and Seleucidan. These broad time divisions were in part correctly dated. What sent the excavators wrong was the fact that in the sites they excavated there are some gaps in occupation. Their technique of excavating was not sufficiently developed to be able to register such gaps.

Petrie's technique of sequence dating was largely adopted and put into practise by his contempories and became, with some refinements, the standard method of archaeologists of all nationalities working in the field in Palestine. Petrie himself was swift to publish his finds, but his recording is slipshod and cumbersome. Methods of recording were improved, but a basic mistake in technique, that of digging down in arbitrary levels of 50 cms or more, was inherited as a law of the Medes and Persians by the vast majority of this pupils and successors, to the total detriment of archaeological progress. The origin of this method was that Petrie believed that on an Egyptian town site it was possible to equate the accumulation of material with a specific time-scale. This idea while perhaps tenable in the specialised context of a site covered by wind blown sand is quite irrelevant on a site composed of generations of decayed and collapsed mud-brick buildings. An Eastern city is not a pastry cook's prize layer cake, one smooth horizontal level following on another. It is an organic object, spreading and diminishing "constantly in a state of differential destruction and construction. Individual building sites rise above their neighbours: the town site itself rises and assumes the contour of a hill: buildings on its slopes are contempory with buildings on its summit. A doorway or a potsherd may be found at one spot 10 ft.

below a doorway or a potsherd of precisely the same date at another spot" [1]). This all important data is completely lost if finds are mechanically recorded from arbitrary levels, such as the top of a wall or from a datum line so many feet above sea level cf. fig. 1.

The student of Palestinian archaeology must remember that practically all the work done to the end of the Mandate in 1948 has followed this illogical and outdated method.

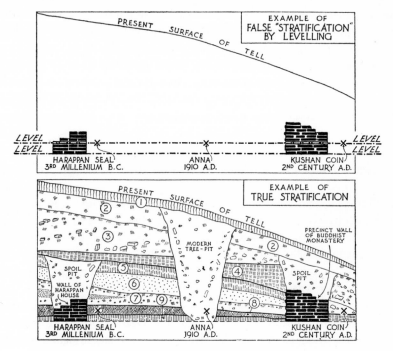

Fig. 1.   Diagrams illustrating the stratigraphy of a city-mound (below) and the fallacy of recording by mechanical levels (above) Wheeler, 'Archaeology from the Earth', fig. 11.

THE ARCHITECT-ARCHAEOLOGISTS

This group is typified by its adherence to the old Classical archaeologists who were working largely on stone built sites, perhaps only partly covered with earth. For them, as for the Petrie followers, walls, paved floors and the like are all important. Objects found within a certain complex of walls are dated alike without a close

---

[1]) Wheeler, Archaeology from the Earth, Oxford p. 53.

regard for the earth filling of that complex. The site's history is recorded by the architect, not by an analysis of all the deposits which ought to be the director's or archaeologist's responsibility. This method can be used with a fair measure of safety in smaller stone-built sites like Qumran, the findspot of the Dead Sea Scrolls, but it can never be entirely reliable. Very often the writers of excavation reports state that various buildings could not with certainty be attributed to a stratum, and that many objects found outside buildings are of uncertain provenance. This shows that excavation outside buildings went on in the Petrie-fashion, without a proper analysis of the earth deposits. Amongst the sites where excavations of this type took place are Tell Abu Hawam, Tell Ajjul, Beth-Shan, Beth-Shemesh, Tell Fara on the Wadi Ghazzeh, Gezer, Gibeah, Jericho (Sellin's and Garstang's excavations), Megiddo, Tell Nasbeh, Samaria (Harvard excavations), Shechem (Sellin's excavations).

Stratigraphical Excavators

This method of excavating, which has been the norm for more than half a century in parts of Europe and England, is only very slowly penetrating into archaeological circles in Palestine. In the discussions about method, found in articles about Palestinian archaeology [1]) after the Jericho excavations from 1952-1958, this method is often misrepresented. The difference between the modern method and older ones can be summarized as follows. In the old systems the deposits of a tell are divided in levels or strata by dividing the stone buildings (or foundations) and clearly recognisable street levels from higher and lower deposits. Usually the height of many points of a stratum is measured, and wherever the attribution to a certain stratum is doubtful, the pottery finds are used as a criteria for attribution to a stratum. Between buildings there are often 'empty spaces', filled with earth deposits, and here the attribution to a stratum is done by the absolute height of the deposits. There are many variations possible in these systems, but to a certain extent they are all more or less artificial. On the other hand there is a basic principle in modern archaeology, derived from geology, that stratigraphy cannot be studied by slicing a tell in horizontal layers only, but that the true nature of the various deposits only becomes clear if the deposits are also studied in vertical cuts. Whereas in the earlier

---

[1]) Cf e.g. E. G. Wright, *J.B.L.*, Vol. 77, 1958, p. 41.

systems the weak point is always the vagueness of the upper and lower limits of each level, in modern archaeology these limits can be exactly fixed. Modern archaeology cannot accept a definition of the findspot of a cylinder seal as follows: 3 feet NE of the E corner of the foundations of wall X, as one often finds in publications. This sort of description indicates a vacuum. Ancient remains of human occupation however do not consist of remains of buildings interrelated by empty quarters. One or more vertical cuts through a stratum will reveal on the sections how the bedlines of the deposits in the 'empty quarters' run, and to which stratum the deposits belong. Hence a proper recording of the stratigraphy demands a three dimensional recording: drawings of vertical sections as well as ground plans. In fact, relations between soil deposits and between stone structures and soil deposits can only be recorded in drawings of vertical cuts. And just as with ground plans of houses, these vertical sections have to be properly i.e. professionally drawn.

The old methods include an accurate horizontal planning of building remains, but show a considerable lack of recording of the third dimension, the depth of the levels. Modern methods of excavation consider the third dimension equally important and add to the study of the building remains the study of all the soil deposits to determine their origin and nature. When studying the excavations of Tell en-Nasbeh one will find that practically all the buildings have been put on one single plan, owing to the fact that the excavators failed to establish the chronological sequence in which they were built. What ought to have been a stereo-photograph is turned into a flat picture without any depth. Needless to say it is in many cases impossible to tell whether the objects have been rightly attributed to a certain stratum or not.

To illustrate the difference in method we reproduce here some section drawings that occur in Palestinian excavation reports. A glance at Fig. 2 (Petrie's section from Tell el-Ajjul, 1938) immediately reveals its uselessness. Walls hang in mid-air, totally unrelated one to another, and no floor levels are shown, let alone pits, post stones, sunken courtyards or any of the features which crop up so frequently n a Near Eastern dig.

Fig. 3 is no better although the excavator Albright has attempted to describe the different periods found. The stratigraphy is not based on the analysis of deposits, but on the combination of finds and the

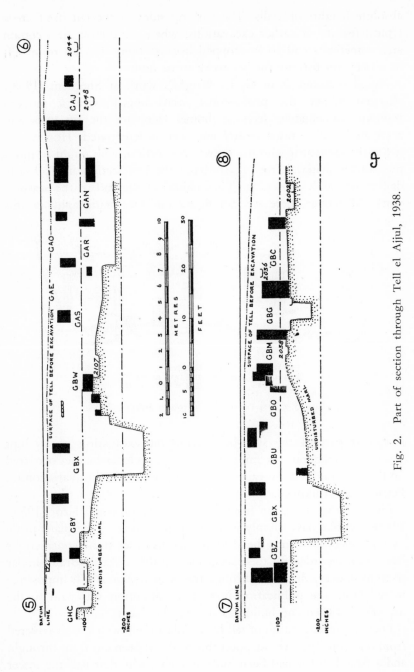

Fig. 2. Part of section through Tell el Ajjul, 1938.

absolute heights of walls. The curving sides of the cut itself are a typical feature of earlier excavations, where excavation in a certain area sometimes had to be stopped because there was no room left in a deep pit for any further work to be done.

Fig. 4 is taken from G. E. Wright's work at Shechem (1958). At first glance the professional archaeologist with a modern training immediately feels at home. Here are the tip lines and associated walls drawn clearly and well differentiated. However it is not the excavator who has drawn this section, who ought to interpret all his material from it, studying the live section meticulously day by day as it grows, but his architect at the end of the season's work. Moreover, here we can figure out the stratigraphy of this

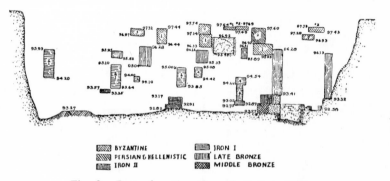

Fig. 3.   Part of section through Bethel, 1939.

particular part of the site, but during the excavation no attempt was made to separate the finds from the various levels as they occurred on the drawing. The so-called Reisner-Fisher method (a variation on Petrie's) was followed.

Fig. 5 shows a section from Yadin's excavations at Hazor (1955). These sections have simply been reconstructed from the plans made by the surveyors. Since the absolute depths of all stone contructions have been recorded on the plans, one can just as easily draw similar sections in every direction through the excavated area! It is impossible to tell from the publication how much attention was paid to the deposits between the buildings during the excavation.

During the excavation of tell Deir 'Allā a town wall was discovered from the Iron Age. At one point this wall had been cut right through, and a round tower had been built in such a way that half the tower was outside this wall, and the other half inside. Our first impression

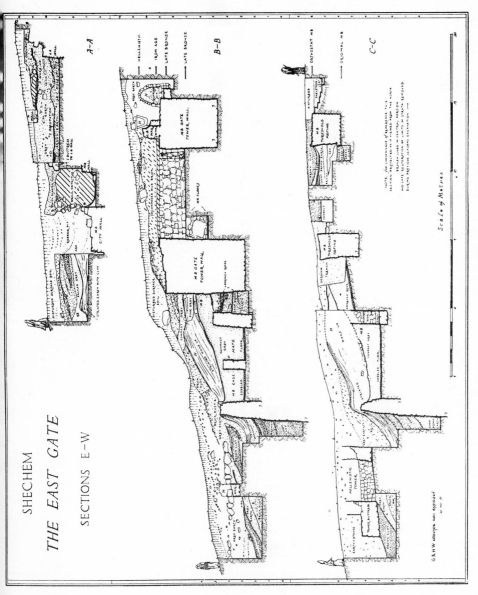

Fig. 4. Section through the East Gate, Shechem, 1957.

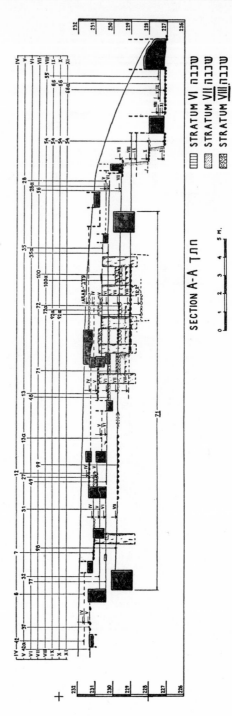

SECTION A-A חתך

STRATUM VI שכבה
STRATUM VII שכבה
STRATUM VIII שכבה

0 1 2 3 4 5 M.

Fig. 5.   Part of section through Hazor, 1955.

was that this tower, the remains of which were immediately under the present surface of the tell, was a later addition to the wall, although we could not explain the fact that half the round tower was inside the line of the wall. However, the study of two cross sections, one across the wall and one across the tower itself, and a section which linked the two, showed that the tower was built after the wall had become a ruin and belonged to a later wall built on a slightly different line from the earlier one, which in that area of the tower had disappeared. This was owing partly to erosion, and partly to mediaeval Arabic graves which had been dug there in great quantities. The builders of the round tower cut into the existing slope of the tell in order to make space for the tower, and during this operation cut right through the earlier wall, which was in that time already buried in its own debris. As found, the tower fitted perfectly well into the earlier wall. One can only guess how much evidence is lost where the study of the soil deposits is neglected.

Fig. 6 shows the fruit of Miss Kenyon's real stratigraphical work at Jericho [1]). The site at Jericho (Tell es-Sultan) has in the past been subjected to two major field expeditions using the sequence-dating method with arbitrary levels, and stress on the architectural remains. Miss Kenyon's stratigraphical method, differing in no substantial way to that employed by her in her work on Roman sites in Britain or North Africa, or that of her colleagues at home (cf. Fig. 7) or on the Continent [2]), was greeted as a revolutionary and while admirable, yet over-laborious way of research by some other excavators in Palestine.

As will be shown in Ch. IV, the work recently done by Miss Kenyon at Jericho has proved that Garstang's reconstruction of the fall of Jericho at the arrival of Joshua [3]) was completely based on the defective methods used by Garstang at Tell es-Sultan. Since his conclusions have been extensively used by Old Testament scholars for fixing the date of the conquest [4]), this is a perfect example to illustrate our plea for the critical study of excavation reports by O.T. scholars. In the meantime, the student who has to acquire some

---

[1]) See Ch. IV, p. 73. A comparison of Miss Kenyon's results with those obtained by J. Garstang at the same site and often in adjoining areas shows immediately their great improvement in accuracy resulting from adequate methods.

[2]) Cf. K. M. Kenyon, *Beginning in Archaeology*, London, 1951.

[3]) J. Garstang and J. B. E. Garstang, *The story of Jericho*, London, 1940. Ch. vii.

[4]) H. H. Rowley, *From Joseph to Joshua*, Schweich Lectures, London, 1948, p. 11.

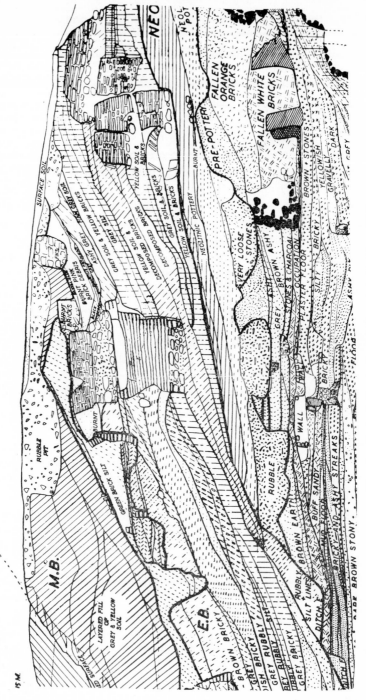

Fig. 6. Part of the section of Trench I, Jericho, 1956.

idea of the results of archaeological research in Palestine, has to be aware of the fact that most of the available excavation reports present him with results that cannot be accepted without a thorough re-examination in the light of modern principles of research. Many published results will have to be revised. The best tool for the critical unravelling of a dig report is logical thought and common sense. This does not mean to say that all evidence and interpretation must be scraped if the methods used are questionable. But it is a warning

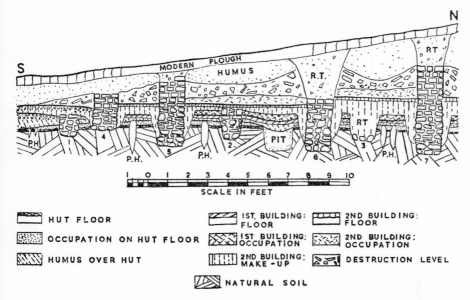

Fig. 7.   Section through a site in which the first occupation is represented by a hut with wooden posts. This was succeeded by a period of abandonment in which humus accumulated. A house was then built with a metalled road along the south side. This first was dismantled, its walls being partly robbed to their bases and was succeeded by a second house. Above the decay of the second house humus accumulated, and the area was eventually ploughed. K. M. Kenyon 'Beginning in Archaeology', Fig. 2.

which will be a recurrent theme in this book, that because the so-called 'facts' of Biblical archaeology are often no firmer than some 'facts' of literary interpretation of the Bible, the often brilliant re-constructions and interpretations of history have to be challenged. It is not lack of intelligence in Palestinian excavators but their lack of an interest in techniques which has made it necessary to write this book.

While dealing with the history of excavations, we cannot conclude this chapter without referring to those Palestinian scholars
who, although they were not necessarily excavators, have influenced
generations of archaeologists by their sound judgement and great
knowledge of the country, its antiquities and their related studies.
The late Père H. Vincent was one of the greatest of their ranks.

CHAPTER TWO

METHOD OF STUDY

There are three cardinal points to remember when studying excavation reports:

1. That due to early or outdated excavation techniques quite a lot of important information about stratigraphy was never recovered. Hence buildings and objects may sometimes have been attributed to a certain level without evidence to prove that the attribution is right.

2. Various levels may have been mixed and published as one single level.

3. That in cases where a destruction of a town is attributed by the excavators to a certain known historical event, the arguments sometimes need careful re-examination.

Thus the uncritical acceptance of field reports is no longer possible. Rowley's study *From Joseph to Joshua* is a very good illustration of this point. The second part, an astoundingly comprehensive study of the literary evidence for the date of the Exodus and Conquest has deservedly given this book a high reputation. In the first part he deals inter alia with the archaeological evidence that was available in 1948. This he accepts literally from the excavation reports, as he would not accept a textual argument. 'Excavation has provided factual evidence that must be accepted without question. Nevertheless the interpretation of the evidence is a different matter. The same evidence is often very differently interpreted by different archaeologists and even the same archaeologist may vary from time to time the conclusions he draws from it!' [1]. The crux of the matter is that often the evidence given is by no means factual and it is not only the interpretation of what is found which must be scrutinized, but also the way in which it was found. Because Rowley accepts these 'facts', he bases his extra-Biblical evidence on uncertain premises.

There are two ways of checking and correcting the finds mentioned in older publications. Either by cross reference with soundly dated objects, or by returning to a given site and re-excavating it.

---

[1] H. H. Rowley, *o.c.*, p. 2.

Palestinian archaeologists are busy with both methods at the moment. Shechem, Jericho and Hazor are all sites where new excavations have been opened up since the end of the Mandate.

Let us take Shechem as an example. E. Sellin, in the first excavations 1926-1927 uncovered a large public building [1]) (see fig. 8), and called it the *Haus des Ba'al Berith*; but its use as a temple remained problematical [2]). Some years later the American team at Megiddo found the remains of a building with an almost identical plan. The associated objects found in both buildings were of little help in explaining the use of these buildings and it was suggested that both buildings were forts, not temples. There was as little evidence for the one as for the other. Besides, in both cases the date of origin was not sufficiently established. Since 1956 G. E. Wright has been examining the site again and trying to establish the stratigraphy and chronology of its buildings. It is very difficult indeed to make an intelligent and plausible reconstruction of buildings such as these where the earlier excavators removed the vast majority of the earth both within and outside the walls, thus destroying most of the potential evidence.

This ideal way of checking the evidence is however far too costly, both of time and money to be done in a widespread way, even if the evidence is still there to be found. Nobody can check the upper levels found in Megiddo, because they were completely stripped, like the upper levels of Beth Shan. Thus recently there have been many archaeological studies reconsidering older conclusions based on the internal evidence of dig reports. Those studies are mainly found in recent excavation reports in connection with the discussion of the dates of the excavated strata. A good example of the reconstruction of a site's history is that by Miss Kenyon, published in the P.E.Q. 1951, before her work at Jericho began. She triumphantly proved in her fieldwork what she had deduced logically from Garstang's reports in conjunction with modern knowledge of pottery dating from other sites. Other important studies are her re-dating of the so-called 'Solomonic stables' at Megiddo [3]) and Yadin's work on the dating of the gates of Megiddo and Gezer, based on his work at Hazor [4]). Wright's work on the 'temple' at Megiddo has already been mentioned.

[1]) *Z.D.P.V.* 1926, pp. 309ff, and 1927, pp. 266ff.
[2]) For the discussions see *Z.A.W.* 1933, pp. 156ff.
[3]) cf. *S.S.* III pp. 198ff.
[4]) cf. *Hazor* II, p. 3 note 12 for literature.

This work is, of course, not the first to be done on the re-dating of Palestinian sites. Earlier work was usually based on typological studies. Crowfoot had suggested the Ahab-date for the 'Solomonic' stables at Megiddo in 1940 [1]), based on architectural grounds; J. H. Iliffe had observed the incorrect dating of a tomb group at Fara by the Wadi Ghazzeh, attributed to the Phoenicians by Fl.

Maßstab 1:1000

0   5   10 15 20   30   40   50 m.

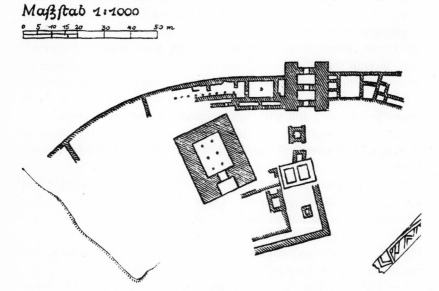

Fig. 8. "Haus des Baal-Berith", at Shechem.

Petrie, whereas Iliffe correctly saw that stylistically the very fine metal objects must date from the Persian period [2]).

The importance of the present trend in the re-examination of Palestinian sites and objects is that the work is being based on the evidence from the soil, the stratigraphical contours, and not solely by the more chancy criteria of style and structure. The rest of this chapter is concerned with showing how the new criteria can be applied to the study of a given object.

The reader will find in the excavation reports mention of the excavated strata of which the tell or city mound consisted and descriptions of architectural remains and a number of objects found in those strata or levels. The date of the beginning and end of each successive

---

[1]) *P.E.Q.* 1940, pp. 132ff.
[2]) *Q.D.A.P.* IV, pp. 182ff.

age or period of the city's life, deduced by signs of destruction, levelling or rebuilding, and change in pottery forms are usually given. Often however one will look in vain for a proper description of each level, its limits and the non-architectural elements of which it consists, Thus the question arises: what is a stratum, how did it build up or grow, and how is it separated from upper and lower strata.

If a town is being excavated the following elements will probably come to light sooner or later: the town wall, the gateway, some dwelling houses, streets, perhaps a large public building. The strata are by no means always divided by a thick level of ash of a destruction, though this is sometimes the case. There is also little chance of finding all the elements of a certain date on the same level. One has only to walk through the city of London to illustrate the case. St Paul's stands on a hill with both nineteenth and twentieth century houses on an absolute level with its walls. Its foundations and those of the nearby twentieth century offices are both sunk into Roman levels.

How then can one hope to separate these complicated facts and arrive at a sound interpretation? There is one very simple guiding principle, often forgotten both by excavators and readers of their reports: at all times in the life of a tell there was an existing surface. Human activities and natural agents may change the surface, but the result is always a new surface.

For instance: The owner of a one roomed house decides to build a second room in his courtyard. He digs the foundation trenches, thus changing the contours of the surface. He then builds the room and lays a floor of cobbles, slightly higher than the courtyard, to prevent flooding in the rainy season. Again the surface is changed. After some time this room collapses, and a thick layer of decayed mud bricks covers the cobbled floor and part of the courtyard: another change of the surface. If this is followed by a general destruction of the city, the surface will again change, and subsequent settlers will level off the ruins, dig out foundation stones, make storage bins etc., by which the surface is again changed.

Stratigraphic research in a tell reconstructs the history of the ever-changing surface, and makes a three dimensional recording of it. If this is properly done, the limits of each level can be exactly fixed, and inside each level the alterations or subdivisions can be shown.

The study of the growth, or rather development of the surface, enables the archaeologist to establish the relative age of each level and of the subdivisions of the levels. He finds that a storage pit was dug simultaneously with the erection of a mudbrick house, and a second storage pit shortly before the house was ruined.

The surveyor of an expedition plans all the various building and digging activities found in each level on plans. He cannot however plan the development of the surface on horizontal plans. Vertical section drawings are needed to record the third dimension. The surveyor plans a house, but the archaeologist 'plans' the position of the collapsed walls and roof, the fill of a bin and the growth of street levels on his section drawings.

Theoretically speaking, every single deposit of earth, clay, ash, stones or any other material, encountered during the excavation, can be recorded and the time sequence established. This means that all the various architectural remains can also be properly fixed in the excavator's time scale.

The relation between various buildings can only satisfactorily be established by means of baulks. Pl. IV a. These are strips of earth, usually a meter wide, crossing the selected area at regular intervals. They are left unexcavated, and show in their vertical sides or sections the relations between the building levels in the area. As the excavators dig down on both sides of the baulk, it assumes the shape of a wall and the site supervisor will leave it there as a guide and check to the interpretation of the strata and subdivisions until he feels quite confident that he has all the information it can give him. He then clears it away after a section drawing has been made (a photograph is usually perfectly useless) Pl. IV, in order to get an undisturbed view of the area as a whole. The great advantage of a baulk is its mobility. A baulk can be left, cut or cleared away at any point where problems arise which need careful checking. They can be used to link different buildings or to tie up walls within a room. Fig. 9 shows in section the later part of the history of two rooms, their adjoining walls and the floor levels excavated at the site of Deir 'Allā in 1961. The various stages can be recorded on plans, but the development is shown in this one drawing of a vertical section.

Instead of applying this fairly simple system,[1] most Palestinian excavators have tried to establish the relationship of various elements in any one level and the relations of the main strata by means of typology of the pottery and other finds [2]). There is, of course, a place

[1] It needs a proper training before one can 'read' sections in the earth.
[2] See Wheeler, *o.c.*, pp. 37f. where Palestinian archaeology is called 'that unfailing source of cautionary examples..'

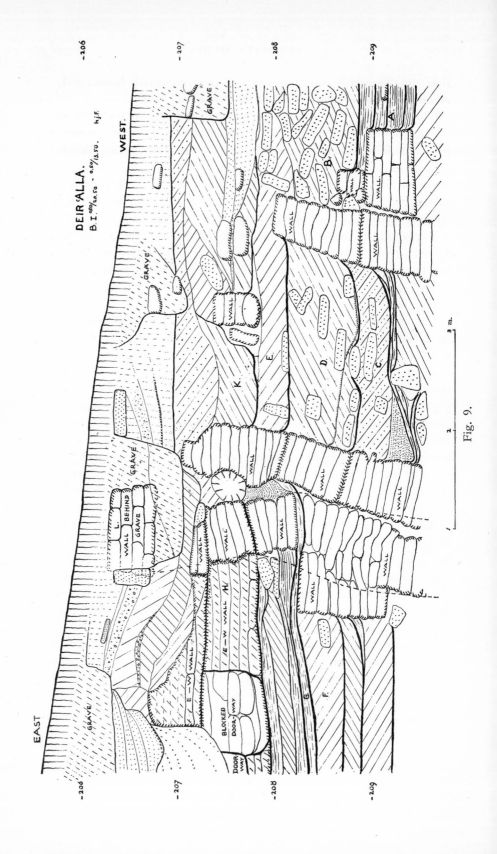

Fig. 9.

for typologies, but these must come after the levels have been securely established on independent evidence.

The following is a perfect example of the old method. In the Amenophis Temple at Beth-Shan a number of rooms are listed in Vol. II, Part I, as forming part of the temple complex. In one of these, Room 1105 'to the North of the temple' a bright yellow glazed bowl was found [1]). It is listed with the Amenophis III pottery inspite of its glaze which is a mediaeval ceramic development, and in spite of the fact that the excavators had their doubts about this cuckoo in the nest. They describe it as 'unique' and add: 'The room in which it was found showed no sign of disturbance or we should have been inclined to regard it as an instrusive piece of Arab pottery.' Which indeed it was.

There are two possible explanations. Perhaps a pit, dating from Arabic times was dug right down into the L.B.A. levels but the excavators failed to recognise the disturbance, (mixed finds) because they never cleaned the floor surfaces properly, nor were there the necessary baulks, or perhaps one of the local labourers 'found' this piece there, which he probably picked up from a field hoping to receive bakshish for a good find. Where this system of bakshish for special finds is followed, coins can even be found in pre-coinage levels.

This shows that an object ought to be studied as part of the whole original context. The context should establish the (relative) date and the phase of the tell when the object was in use and what its use was.

The context in this case is a single stratum or a tomb group. The stratum must first be studied to see what its relation is to the layers immediately above and below it. For instance, is there an ash layer covering the stratum in question? If so, does this represent a major disaster such as the destruction of the city, or is this a local accident of a house burning down? Is the stratum in question undisturbed, or have pits of a later date been dug into it? What is the character of the soil that the stratum is resting on? Perhaps it is sterile, wind blown sand or water-laid clay indicating that a site was abandoned for a while. All these general points and many others must first be taken into consideration. In many of the older publications these questions can only be partly answered because it was not then considered necessary to publish a site in such detail and

---

[1]) *O.c.*, Pl. LXI, 16.

owing to the techniques used many of these points were overlooked. Observe the following strange definition of stratigraphy [1]): 'The conventional use of 'strata' in the analysis of the formation of a mound suggests a history divisible into static phases in each of which the life and culture of the last are definitely superseded. The history of fact is not so divided. In Jerusalem to-day a twelfth-century building stands in good condition and in active use while its twentieth-century neighbour, already a rubbish heap, will soon be a ruin. Similar conditions doubtless marked the evolution of an ancient site, and a certain complexity in the structural remains is the result. Stratigraphy is the attempt to simplify or schematize that complexity so that it may be used to co-ordinate intelligibly the associated material. Where the architecture has little intrinsic merit the plans are still necessary as the framework within which the essential historical relations of one object to another are preserved....' Stratigraphy was often an hypothesis of work instead of an existing fact which the excavator must study.

Once the stratum has been isolated the objects found together in it should be collected together. Sometimes whole groups are published together, but more often the various objects are separated into typologies such as: weapons, cooking pots, stone bowls, etc. If a true picture of the context is to be seen, these typologies must be broken down and the objects re-assembled. This is a laborious, tedious job. There seems no escape from it, and the simplest method is to sketch the objects from the publication on to one large sheet. If a really large reconstruction work is contemplated such as work on Megiddo, where an enormous mass of material was found, then it is quicker to make photographic copies of the plates, cutting out the objects required and pasting them onto file cards. While doing this, one should keep in mind that objects labelled 'from debris' may easily be of a different date than objects that definitely are found on floor levels.

Once the group is re-assembled the student should look out for the most characteristic pieces for dating. The charts on figs. 13, 15, 16, 24, 25, 30, 31, 39 give such groups with the most characteristic forms of pottery and other objects. Comparison with objects from other publications is necessary to get a dating as close as possible. However, this needs comparative material from sites that have been

---

[1]) *Q.D.A.P.* Vol. IV, p. 2.

properly excavated. In order to save himself time the student will obviously search for comparative material in those publications which he knows to be most reliable before turning to the older works. This comparative study should establish the date when the object was made and whether it was used widely over the whole country or only locally. This poses more questions. If locally, was it for a special industry or cult? If widespread, does it show regional differences or are the objects so similar as to suggest a central industry? Where then was this industry? Is it imported or was it a home product?

Once one object or group of objects have been securely dated in this way, then they themselves become extremely valuable for dating associated objects for which no close comparisons can be found.

Without a fairly close dating of objects one should never try to associate any archaeological finds with Biblical evidence. Objects, whose context are not known, are archaeologically speaking practically worthless. Every archaeological expedition produces some objects which cannot safely be assigned to any stratum, such as the stray surface finds on the unexcavated part of the site which a heavy fall of rain may reveal, e.g. coins or beads.

A chronological classification based on the development of forms is only misleading if it is not firmly grounded in the stratigraphical study of each individual find. As far as pottery is concerned not only the rims, handles, bases and any decorated pieces have diagnostic value, but the treatment of the pot and its finish and the mixing of the clay or way of firing it in the kiln have to be taken into consideration. This limits the possibilities of the student and the scope of this book at the same time. One cannot learn about pottery properly unless one has handled a great mass of pottery fragments [1]).

The reader will by now have seen how much stress is laid on stratigraphical work. Perhaps in order to make its uses clearer it will not be out of place to give some more illustrations of stratigraphical problems and answers.

Let us take a simple example of a ruined house and try to set it in its context in the ruined city mound. It is a one roomed house, built in a traditional manner: four foundation trenches were dug, packed with river stones and the walls built on top from mud-bricks. There is a door in one wall without a threshold, and perhaps a small opening in another to provide a little light and to let out the smoke

---

[1]) See Appendix.

of the fire. The roof was constructed of some horizontal beams over which were laid reeds and on top of them a good layer of thick clay. At a certain moment disaster overtook this town. Houses were burnt down, including this dwelling and the site was left unoccupied for a long time.

In fig. 10 we can see the remains of the house in section. This section is but a part of a larger one showing the history of this piece of ground before the house was built, (an earlier destruction level), and what happened later, after the town was once more inhabited. In the excavation level A was first found and was eventually re- cognised as debris of the collapsed roof. Under A were found the charred remains of the roof beams. A lay on debris B from the collapsed walls, and B lay on C, the level comprising the earth and

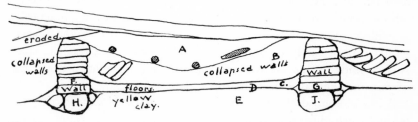

Fig. 10.   Section through a ruined mud-brick dwelling, as it was drawn in the field.

kitchen waste of the original floor D. D lay on E, the top of an older destruction level. There were only small fragments of walls F and G still in their original positions. But the foundation trenches H and J were clearly recognisable.

In this schematic section of a single room one can thus see by analysis at least three different levels whose material remains could consist of three different age groups. These levels are: 1, A, B, F and G; 2, C and 3, E, H and J. The first group A, B, F and G will have fewer objects, in particular potsherds. This is the clay from which the house was built. This clay was generally taken from a nearby place so that old fragments of pottery dating from every earlier period may be incorporated in the bricks used for building. If these walls or the roof were not partially or completely renewed during the life time of the house, these fragments are of course older than the time of the building of the house. The group E, H and J consisting of the foundation trenches and the level directly below the floor will have sherds almost certainly dating from the settlement which directly preceded the building of the house, as well as the few sherds of pots broken at the time that the house was built. These sherds give us the terminus post quem of the building. Separated by the floor from E is the occupation level C consisting of all the objects which got dropped on the floor and trodden into it and the household objects in use at the time of the disaster. These objects give us the possibility of fixing the general period in which the house was destroyed.

While excavating down through Iron Age levels at Tell Deir 'Allā, the number of Late Bronze Age sherds found in clay deposits of destroyed walls increased steadily while we approached the L.B. strata. In the lower I.A. levels we also found Chalcolithic sherds. This is an indication that the I.A. inhabitants took clay from the slopes of the tell outside the town wall in Chalcolithic tip-lines to build their mud-brick houses. Later in the I.A. these slopes were covered under a thick deposit of I.A. debris, from the successive collapsed town walls. But in an earlier phase the L.B. material was still sufficiently near the surface to be dug up in the clay quarries. Similarly the L.B. debris contained stray Chalcolithic sherds. This shows that clay debris is bound to have earlier material in it which can easily be mixed with material used for dating the actual building, especially when the difference in time is less, such as 9th century material in 8th century buildings.

Had this house been excavated in the assumption that everything from the bottom of the foundation trenches to the top of the stumps of the walls belongs to the same level, (as was frequently done in Palestine in the past), than at least two periods would have been mixed together.

This particular example shows a really very simple archaeological situation. There are in reality scores of possible variations. There are occasions when only the foundation trenches remain to witness that a house once stood there. Later generations rob the stone for building their own houses. In this case the fill found in the foundation trenches will date from the time of the destruction of the house or later. The house may be rebuilt before the debris has been levelled so that the new floor lies only a little higher than the old one. In later times pits may be dug through the building which fill in again slowly. Erosion from the higher parts of the tell may fill up the spaces between the ruined walls with earlier, contemporary or later material. The excavator has to contend with all these possibilities as he tries to analyse his levels.

Excavation reports often present the student with such mysterious situations as rooms with no floors. Clearly, as every house or room ever built and used has had a floor (and in mud brick buildings with beaten earth floors, often a whole succession, see fig. 9) the fact is that the presence of floors has not been observed. Floors are often very badly worn or partially destroyed by house alterations and in general obscured by the accumulation of earth fill and debris which piles up on them after a house has been destroyed or abandoned. But as the objects found just below and just above a floor level are of the greatest importance for fixing the terminus post quem and the date of destruction the student will readily grasp how important it is that each floor level should be traced and recorded. This can be done by leaving cross baulks in the room which is being excavated, so that even if a floor has been destroyed against the wall or in one half of the room, it will show up somewhere in section in the baulk. The excavator who writes that 'no floors were found' means in fact that he has allowed his workmen to clear out a room completely down to the foundations without taking due precautions for the recovery of what is, after all, the part of the house which takes the greatest wear and tear.

An example of this is to be found in the large building at New Testament Jericho (tell Abū el-'Alâyiq). Some rooms were reported without floors [1]). The probable explanation for the apparent absence of floors seems to be that after the building was no longer in use it was robbed for the use of a near-by structure, probably a Byzantine Church. The walls had been robbed of their ashlar blocks. In other rooms of the same building mosaic floors were found overlying cobbles; so it is likely that the other floors were also made of mosaics, fit for re-use in a church or similar building. This could have been established by a cut right across the rooms instead of all along the walls [2]). Following the walls round, instead of digging up to them is a well known and disastrous archaeological mistake. Pl. VI.

Other vague indications of findspots occur, such as: 'found in debris West of room...', and 'at the bottom of room...' [3]) Here the case is in fact clearer: during excavation no attention has been paid to the stratigraphy of 'empty quarters', spaces between buildings,

---

[1]) *AASOR* XXXII-XXXIII, 1952-4. The Excavations at Herodian Jericho 1951. J. B. Pritchard (1958), p. 4-6, Room 3, 7, 8, 23, 24, 29, 30, 32.
[2]) *V.T.* Vol. VIII, pp. 443-445.
[3]) See *e.g. A.A.S.O.R.* XXXIV-V, p. 16 'at the bottom of room B'.

walls that did not seem to form a proper room, etc. As we have seen already, stratification of sites is never limited to architectural remains, but is quite naturally found in every inch of all the accumulated material. Buildings have often been treated as islands in an amorphous sea of debris. Proper analysis of the debris will show the various surfaces and the accumulation on them, by means of which the buildings can be put in their time sequence of origin and destruction. And not only the architectural remains, but also the objects found outside buildings, which fell down at a certain time on an existing surface and remained there until they were excavated. And last but not least, there are the soil deposits themselves, which up till now have often been considered as a sort of wood-wool in which the precious objects were packed. The soil needs the same careful study, recording and sometimes chemical analysis before it can be disposed of on the dump. All field work deals with three dimensions in its totality.

In the report on the excavation at Tell en-Nasbeh the following is stated: 'There was no clear stratification during a good part of the period covered because there was no complete destruction and rebuilding at any one time' [1]. Wheeler comments on this: 'This, of course, is nonsense; by 'stratification' the writer quoted means merely 'continuous building levels' oblivious of the no less important layers which on any site may be expected to supplement and inter-relate phases of actual constructions. The fact is that the observer had simply failed to observe' [2].

Plans published in archaeological reports are sometimes darkened by the number of the so-called 'absolute heights' (or depths) of floors, foundations and tops of walls or other elements recorded on them cf. Fig. 5. As those plans can be fitted in the right order on top of each other, vertical sections can be drawn from those plans in every direction by the surveyor at his desk. Such sections miss the essential point: the recording of the observed deposits of soil and the relations between the architectural remains. They can tell us no more about the elevation of various elements than horizontal plans and too much of the evidence of the soil has been omitted for the establishment of relations.

There is no need to list here all the pitfalls known to lurk in every

---

[1] W. Badé. *Tell en-Nasbeh.*
[2] Wheeler, *o.c.*, p. 44.

Palestinian site which has been excavated, for, of every one known there are probably two unknown. Obviously excavation techniques will improve. In ten or twenty years time laboratory methods of dating finds will probably give us a far closer dating than can be obtained now. Meanwhile it is the student's duty to measure the reports and discoveries made in Palestine by the most efficient methods now known. It is a sad fact that very few excavations could or can pass this test with flying colours. It is in Palestine 'where more sins have probably been commited in the name of archaeology than on any commensurate portion of the earth's surface' [1].

Apart from urging the student to watch out vigilantly for the stratification or lack of it in reports the writers would suggest that he might also ask himself these following questions when looking through a dig report. Are there adequate photographs of the areas and objects found? Do the photos of the areas under excavation show piles of earth dumped beside and trickling down into the area and scores of workmen teaming around in that area? Compare plate VIIa with plate VIIb. Are the sides of the cuts straight and clean? Are walls or pillars left in situ on crumbling columns of earth while work progresses below them, or is there a general impression of clean tidy work? Pl. Vb. Is there a meter pole to show scale or must the reader rely on guessing the height of a young Arab boy standing stiffly to attention? Does the reader find drawings of the pottery as well as photographs and is there a proper description? These and similar questions will make it possible for the reader to decide from the outset how much authority he can place on a given publication or detailed study and which he must treat with a pinch of salt.

It will be clear after what has been said above, that the beginner in Biblical archaeology ought not to try to tackle any of the older publications of excavations, but should start on the recent ones. Besides, what holds good for the excavation reports also applies to many studies of special subjects. Articles and monographs on archaeological subjects sometimes show (even up to the present day [2]) quite the same lack of understanding of stratigraphy, precision and accuracy when discussing archaeological finds or levels, and consequently the conclusions are not reliable.

---

[1] Wheeler, *o.c.*, p. 16.
[2] *V.T.* Vol. XI p. 100 and pp. 471ff.

It is also clear then, that this introduction to modern Biblical archaeology can only attempt to give students the right ideas about the study of the results of archaeological research and not more than that. No pure armchair archaeology leads to original work. The first hand sources of the trade are only found in the field [1]).

---

[1]) The identification of ancient sites is a special subject not dealt with in this book.

CHAPTER THREE

A SHORT OUTLINE OF THE HISTORY
OF PALESTINE IN ARCHAEOLOGICAL PERIODS

One of the greatest successes of Palestinian archaeology as a whole has been the gradual discovery of the cultures which flourished in Palestine before the coming of the Israelites. To the average reader of the Bible the history of Palestine takes its first vague beginnings in the age of the Patriarchs and until comparatively recently not much was known about the history of the country than the pure fact that peoples had lived there before the Israelites came. While the discovery and decipherment of ancient texts related to the history of the great civilisations in the Near East pushed the limits of the historical period in that part of the world back into the fourth millennium B.C., the knowledge of Palestinian history was only indirectly affected as no such important written documents were found in her soil.

Thus from lack of historical information proper about historical events which could enable archaeologists to identify them *e.g.* to fix absolute dates for the destructions of towns that they excavate etc., the archaeology of Palestine resembles in many respects prehistoric archaeology. We know, for instance, that Lachish was an Israelite town, that it was besieged in 587 B.C. by the troops of Nebucadnezar and captured. Part of this town has been excavated and identified [1]). However although the site of Lachish was inhabited, from the beginning of urban civilization right through the Bronze Age we know no more about the site than excavation can tell us and up till now very little work has been done on the earlier strata [2]). On the other hand, even if more was known about Palestine from hieroglyphic or cuneiform documents, only excavations could tell us about the material cultures which flourished and perished in that country. Many traces of the cultures of 'prehistoric' or preliterary Palestine have been found through excavations, and it is at least possible now to sketch in outline the history of those cultures

[1]) cf. *Lachish* III, Text, pp. 38ff.
[2]) cf. *Lachish* IV, Text, Ch. I.

and some of their main characteristics. For convenient reference the main periods have been named after the material which was supposedly mainly used for making tools in each epoch. The names and the sequence of these periods, the 'three period system', come from Christian Thomson, Director of the Danish National Museum at Copenhagen, published in 1836 [1]): Stone Age, Bronze Age and Iron Age. All three periods can be subdivided into three periods with their own characteristics, and transitional periods, whereas yet further divisions have been made necessary by the discoveries of the various cultures that flourished during those times, but were divided both by time and/or space. Palestine is one of the countries where all the main periods are represented.

The 'three period' system has proved very useful, but no such system has yet been generally accepted for the subdivisions, especially those of the second and third periods. This holds both for names of subdivisions and for time scales. There is no unity in the publications, and Iron Age II *e.g.* can be the same as early Iron II (c. 900-600 B.C.) in different systems. Hence the student of archaeological reports will have to translate such names into dates to avoid confusion. Here follow two lists of periods and approximate dates. Both authors of these lists have arrived at their results after a long period of excavations and research. From the second list, which is the more recent one, it will be clear that there are many uncertainties which can only be solved by further excavation. For the Stone Age only the three main subdivisions are given here.

W. F. Albright [2]), who has made a major contribution to our knowledge of Palestinian chronology, arrived at the following time-table:

PALEOLITHIC
MESOLITHIC, c. 6000 (?)
NEOLITHIC, c. 6000 (?)-4500
CHALCOLITHIC, c. 4500-3200

BRONZE AGE:

Early Bronze I 3200-3000 (or earlier)
Early Bronze II 29th century

---

[1]) cf. H. J. Eggers, *Einführung in die Vorgeschichte*, München, 1959, pp. 32ff. This book is recommended for further study of archaeological methods of interpretation.

[2]) Cf. W. F. Albright, *The Archaeology of Palestine*, Penguin Books.

Early Bronze III, minimal date 26th-23rd century
Early Bronze IV (or III B) 23rd-21st century.

TRANSITIONAL STAGE, 21st century:
Middle Bronze I, 21st-19th century
Middle Bronze II, 18th-17th century
Late Bronze I, c. 1550-15th century
Late Bronze II, 14th-13th century

IRON AGE:
Iron Age I, 12th-10th century
Iron Age II, 9th-6th century
Iron Age III, 550-330.

Most of these periods are subdivided in Albright's system, (*e.g.* M.B. II, A, B and C), and these subdivisions roughly coïncide with strata excavated at Tell Beit Mirsim and other sites, like Megiddo. Thus M.B. II C indicates Tell Beit Mirsim Stratum D, covering the 17th and part of the 16th century, or the last Hyksos phase.

It remains to be seen whether these subdivisions can be applied generally in Palestinian archaeology or not. In a period of 150 or two hundred years there will be changes both locally and generally in the objects manufactured, a process which will differ from place to place. Such changes are obvious where a town was several times destroyed within one cultural period, with each destruction level containing the latest phase of the development. But this cannot always be a sound criteria for dating these changes. The upper stratum of Tell Beit Mirsim (A), where during a period of about three centuries no main destruction occured, is a good example of this. From this long period only the pottery from the last decades was found, and although inhabited all the time, Tell Beit Mirsim did not supply any evidence for subdivision over a period of 300 years.

Miss Kenyon's work on the chronology of the earlier periods is mainly based on her excavations of Tell es-Sultan (Jericho). It is also thanks to her work at Samaria that some of the pottery types of the 9th and 8th century B.C. can be closely dated. At Jericho she distinguished 5 phases in the same period as Albright's M.B. II, which illustrates what has been said above about subdivisions. 'Many of these features (i.e. of certain pottery types) have for long been recognised as of chronological significance, but the evidence of the Jericho tombs has enabled more precision to be given to some of the characteristics. Further work will no doubt add a greater precision' [1] Chronological research at Tell es-Sultan benefitted from the possibility of checking archaeological results with C. 14 tests of excavated organic matter from the earliest levels. Miss Kenyon's estimation of the age of the early periods based on archaeological evidence agrees amazingly well with these C. 14 tests. The following is basically the result of archaeological research, and dates confirmed by C. 14 tests are marked (C 14):

PALEOLITHIC until 9th millennium B.C.

MESOLITHIC 8th millennium (C. 14 $\pm$7800 B.C. for Jericho)

NEOLITHIC 7th-first half of 5th millennium B.C. (C. 14 for first pre-ceramic culture at Jericho $\pm$7000 B.C.)

CHALCOLITHIC 4500-3200 B.C.

TRANSITIONAL STAGE, 32nd century B.C.

EARLY BRONZE AGE, 3100-2300, with the possibility that 2300 B.C. is too late for the end of E.B.A. or else there is a yet unknown stage in the second half of the 3rd millennium B.C.

TRANSITIONAL STAGE 2300-1900 B.C. which she calls the Intermediate E.B.—M.B. culture, which is intrusive in Palestine and culturally speaking belongs neither to the foregoing nor to the following period [2]).

MIDDLE BRONZE AGE, 1900-1550 B.C.

TRANSITIONAL STAGE, 1550-1500 B.C.

LATE BRONZE AGE, 1500-1200 B.C.

IRON AGE: Early I and II with the transition in the 9th century.

Jericho will without any doubt become a key site for the chronology of Palestine from Neolithic times until the Late Bronze age, except for the Chalcolithic period which was not sufficiently represented there.

The history of fixed dates in Palestine, dealing with known characters who led their people in peace and war, judged their crimes and offered their sacrifices, fades away when we look back as far as the M.B. All that remains to us is broad cultural history. 'Real' history can be traced back into the Chalcolithic period in Egypt and to similarly early times in Mesopotamia. Thus contemporary Palestinian

---

[1]) K. M. Kenyon, *Archaeology in the Holy Land*, p. 173.

[2]) Also known as the Caliciform culture by Miss O. Tufnell and others.

cultures can be compared and put into the general picture as shown by the history of the greater nations.

PALEOLITHIC

Palestine and Syria are important findspots of various paleolithic cultures [1])

MESOLITHIC

This period is called in Palestine the Natufian, and what evidence there is about this cultural period is an important contribution to the general picture of the struggle of mankind to adept himself to changing conditions. Unlike their 'immediate' predecessors of the late Paleolithic they were hunters of small animals and birds, and fishers. They lived at the end of the last Ice Age and it seems that they were the first to endeavour to coöperate with nature by starting to cultivate land and breed stock. They tried to become independent from the constantly migrating herds of big game.

NEOLITHIC

With regard to Neolithic times Palestine has given most surprising evidence of a highly organised and comparatively sophisticated urban civilisation in the Jordan valley [2]). The completely unexpected discovery of five successive Neolithic stages at Tell es-Sultan [3]) has revolutionised ideas about the Late Stone Age. Here the first discovery was made of two neolithic cultures each with a walled town and a well organised community life, dating from before the invention of pottery making. These cultures may have been so dependent on certain favourable climatic conditions that, as far as we know, they perished when these conditions deteriorated. The earliest known sculpture occurs here with the Jericho plastered skulls.

The earliest known pottery from Palestine comes from a later phase in the Neolithic Age, and has hitherto been found in three places: Jericho, Lachish and Shechem, which points to a wide spread in Palestine. (Cf. Fig. 11).

---

[1]) D. Garrod and R. Neuville, *The Stone Age of Mount Carmel.*

[2]) Also found in Wadi Sueib and near Petra by Miss D. Kirkbride.

[3]) Jericho is the only large tell which has been excavated to bedrock in its core. Early neolithic remains very possibly lie beneath the untouched levels of other mounds.

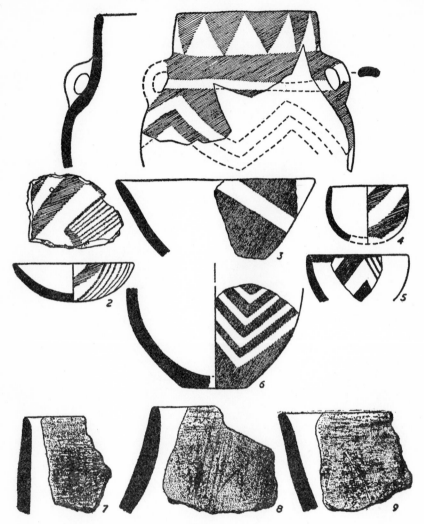

Fig. 11. Neolithic pottery, Jericho.

CHALCOLITHIC

The following period, the Chalcolithic Age is named after the mixed use of metal and stone for the fabrication of tools. There are however more important characteristics of this time. Everywhere in the Near East villages dating from this period have been discovered, although only few of them have been excavated yet. The pottery of the time is very typical and shows a wide development of different

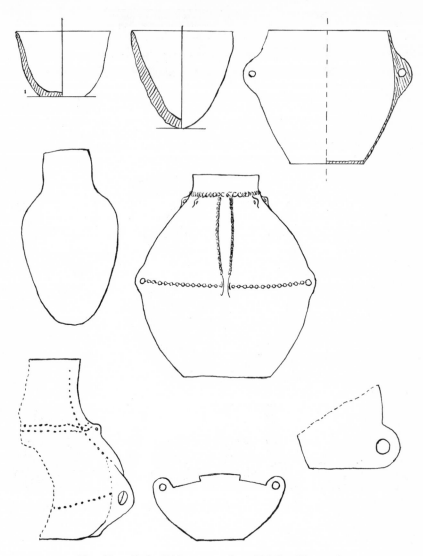

Fig. 12.   Chalcolithic pottery from Teleilat Ghassoul.

shapes. At this time the Jordan valley seems to have been densely populated, and one of the most famous discoveries of this time was Teleilat Ghassoul, east of the Jordan near the Dead Sea (cf. Fig. 12) where mural paintings were discovered [1]).

---

[1]) A. Mallon, R. Koeppel, R. Neuville: *Teleilat Ghassul*, Rome I,1934, II,1940.

Further excavations in the lower levels of well-known Biblical towns may well show that many of them started as Chalcolithic villages. Remains of the period have been found at Megiddo, Samaria Tell el-Far'a, Beth Shan, Shechem, Beersheba and Deir 'Allā. They were agricultural settlements, and since they are also found in regions which are now arid they may well give proof that between 4000 and 3000 B.C. Palestinian mountains were still thickly forested and the important wadi's (seasonal riverbeds) were still permanent streams. In that case the foot hills on the west side of the Jordan valley may still have had a thick humus level.

Transition to the Early Bronze Age

As these settlements were successful, conditions were created for an increase of the population and this led, after the meso-neolithic 'revolutions' [1]) in the ways of life of earlier man, towards a new series of changes in communal life. This development in Palestine ended in widespread urbanisation as in Egypt and Mesopotamia where, as written records show, the first regional kingdoms were built up. With them came the centralisation of power and an increased mutual influence between the various city-states which were the origin of the great civilisations.

It is often thought that the dolmens, many of which still exist on the east side of the Jordan valley, were built in this period but up till now no indications have been found of their date of origin.

By the end of the Chalcolithic age we find in Palestine approximately in the south, the centre and the north three different groups, recognised by the pottery they used, who were the immediate forerunners of the civilisation of the Early Bronze Age [2]). They have been found centred near Jerusalem (Ophel), at Tell el-Far'ah [3]) and in the plain of Esdraelon [4]) (Megiddo, Beth-shan, 'Affula). These finds come mostly from tombs, and are not associated with walled settlements.

The importance of these discoveries is, that we here find the early elements from which the population in Palestine was built up. Since archaeology is still in the process of collecting material about this

---

[1]) G. Childe: *What Happened in History*, Pelican Books, 1950.
[2]) Kenyon, *Archaeology* Ch. 4.
[3]) R. de Vaux in *R.B.* LVI.
[4]) G. E. Wright, *The Pottery of Palestine from the Earliest Times to the End of the Bronze Age*, New Haven , 1937.

time, there is no commonly accepted name for it. E. G. Wright, in his study of the early pottery [1]) has put it in a coherent picture between Chalcolithic and Early Bronze and indicated this period as E.B.I.A. The group from tell el-Far'ah near Nablus is called by the excavator Éneolithic Superieur. The Ophel and Ai material was called late Chalcolithic. According to Miss Kenyon the three groups can be synchronised, mainly from the finds of Père de Vaux at tell el-Far'ah and from tell es-Sultan [2]) (cf. fig. 13) and the period should be distinguished from Chalcolithic proper as well as from the fully developed E.B. and called Proto-Urban, analogous with the Proto-literate

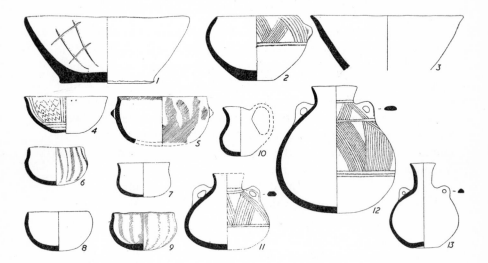

Fig. 13. Proto-Urban pottery forms.

period in Mesopotamia and the Proto-Dynastic period in Egypt. The suggested date for this period is c. 3400 B.C. to 3100 B.C., with a margin probably of a century at either end.

THE EARLY BRONZE AGE

This period occupies most of the third millennium B.C. Dates attributed to the beginning and the end of this period cannot be expressed in exact years. The beginning of the E.B.A. is a slow process, since the fully developed E.B. culture emerges gradually

---

[1]) O.c.
[2]) Kenyon, *Excavations at Jericho* Vol. I, Ch. 2. London, 1960.

from the 'Proto-urban' stage, and the progress seems to have been faster
in the north and the centre of Palestine than in the south. The end
seems to have come about abruptly by the invasion of numerous
nomads who destroyed many cities, but until now it has not been
possible to fix the date more closely than within two centuries.

One of the reasons of this uncertainty is that although excavations
have been carried out on many mounds only a few have reached
the E.B. levels, and most of our information comes either from trial
cuts in one or two corners of mounds, or from tombs. The Proto-
Urban period falls in the end of the fourth millennium B.C., and the
E.B. is fully developed before 3000 B.C., whereas the end of the
E.B. comes somewhere between 2300 and 2100 B.C.

The period has been divided into three (sometimes four) subdivisions based on the study of the pottery [1]) and our main means of
turning the relative sequence dating into an absolute chronology is
by a comparison of finds with Egyptian objects that can be attributed
to the early Dynasties. Up till now most attention has been given to
the chronology of this period, as very little is known about the people
who lived in that age and their ways of life. At Jericho for instance
the defences of the E.B. town were extensively examined, and many
tombs (often reused in later times) were excavated, but on the tell
itself only a very small portion of the town was preserved to be
unearthed. Many of the sites already occupied in the fourth millennium
B.C. continued into the third millennium and gradually became
walled towns, except most of the sites in the Jordan valley and Tell-
en-Nasbeh, Samaria and Shechem (?). Other towns were founded
for the first time in the course of the period, like Tell Beth Mirsim.
Agriculture seems to have been the main occupation of the inhabitants
and the majority of the tools used by the farmers was still made of
flint. Cultural contacts with the North (Byblos) and the South
(Egypt) existed, mainly because a long stretch of the trade route
between the northern lands and Egypt went through the plains of
northern and western Palestine. Nothing suggests that Palestine
was part of a foreign kingdom during this period, nor is there evidence
of a political unity of Palestine itself. It is most likely that Palestine
was divided in city states, and that the towns were still organized
tribally under chiefs.

Our most important evidence for the reconstruction of this time

---

[1]) cf. Wright, *o.c.*

comes mainly from four sites: Tell es-Sultan, where the successive stages of the town walls have been thoroughly studied; Tell el-Far'ah where five successive occupation levels were discovered, belonging to the first half of the third millennium B.C.; et-Tell where an important sanctuary was excavated; and Khirbet Kerak, where for the first time a new type of pottery was found, named after this site, dating from E.B. III.

The many walled cities point to the lack of a strong central government. Even if a confederation of city-states existed, there would have been many reasons for local conflicts, which made the defence of each settlement necessary. The Book of Judges gives a vivid picture of a country without a central government in the beginning of the Iron Age.

Elaborate study of the early tombs near Tell es-Sultan has shown that much erosion, due to deforestation in connection with the claiming of more land for agriculture, took place in the second half of the third millennium B.C. The towns consumed much wood, as the excavations have shown, and the extension of the cultivated areas by cutting the forests caused the erosion of the slopes of the hills. By the deforestation the water table was lowered, and the growing of crops became more and more dependent on sufficient seasonal rainfall. Thus the economic situation may well have deteriorated slowly and the disastrous end of the E.B.A. civilisation in Palestine, brought about by the invasions of warrior nomads, may well have had its deeper roots in the economic situation of the country.

Although very little is known about the religion of the inhabitants, one remarkable find is that of a large temple building at et-Tell [1]). In bare essentials the plan of this temple resembles the description of the temple built by Phoenician architects for King Solomon in Jerusalem more than a millennium later.

The pottery of the period developed out of that of the preceding times, but practically comes to a full stop at the end of the period. This is one of the most striking instances of the change of a culture first indicated by pottery finds. In the E.B. pottery repertoire many improvements in the technique of pottery making are noticeable; the ware becomes thinner and harder; the technique of burnishing the pot before firing it is often applied (Khirbet Kerak ware) and there are indications that turning the pot on a slow wheel was tried.

---

[1]) J. Marquet, *Les Fouilles de 'Ay (Et-Tell)*, Beyrouth, 1949.

In earlier periods Palestinian pottery is found in Egypt, whereas little is known of the importation of pottery from elsewhere into Palestine. From this the deduction can be made that Palestine worked out its own development, little disturbed by events in the neighbouring countries. One can be fairly certain of one thing:

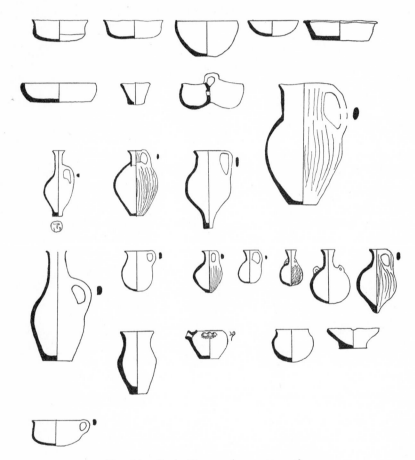

Fig. 14. Early Bronze Age pottery forms.

every now and again Palestine was the target of nomadic incursions from east and north, bringing disasters to towns and crops. The nomadic element does not usually contribute to the culture of a sedentary population, as archaeology clearly shows in the case of the coming of the Israelites. As a result usually no other indications of those invasions are found than the occasional destruction of settlements. The many destructions of the town walls of E.B. Jericho may at least partly be due to such raids.

In sharp contrast to what has been said above about the nomadic invasions the next general cultural period is completely dominated by a nomadic culture. Following the E.B.A. we find in Palestine a lapse of cultural achievement, which forms a real dark age in the history of the country. Sometime after 2300 B.C. nomadic tribes invaded Palestine on a large scale, and put an end to town life. As far as archaeological evidence goes, there is a complete break between the E.B.A. and the Middle Bronze Age, in which no walled towns

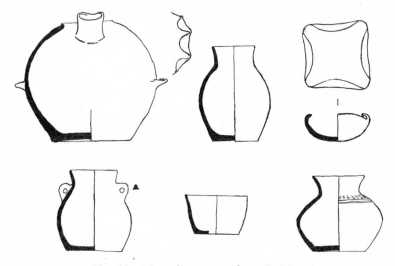

Fig. 15.   Nomadic pottery from Jericho.

existed, and not even what might be called villages have been found. These invasions, thought to have connections with the general disturbances in the Near East, changed the face of the country completely. Instead of town life and agriculture, only nomadic traces have been found in Palestine proper, with their typical burial habits, camping sites and rough shelters. These nomads have been traced in most parts of the country generally through fragments of their distinctive pottery on tells and groups of pottery in tombs. (Fig. 15) After the excavations at Tell Beit Mirsim the pottery was attributed to the M.B.A., although distinguished from the real M.B. shapes. At Megiddo we find the pottery of this group completely mixed with that of the following culture, mainly because no distinction was made, stratigraphically speaking, between occupation levels and their material and tombs found in the same 'absolute' level. It is again at Jericho [1]) that a sharp distinction has been worked out from the preceding and the following eras. Miss Kenyon righlty divides this period from the E.B.A. and the M.B.A., both separate unities culturally which have nothing to do with an intermediate period. This pottery cannot even be called transitional, since it did not develop out of Palestinian traditions. She compares this time with the First Intermediate of Egypt and prefers to call it the Intermediate E.B.—M.B. period[2]). She accepts the suggestion that here for the first time the Amorites came into the country and this would give the first links with Biblical accounts. Yet it is by no means certain that these nomadic tribes were related to or connected with the Amorites. Cultural contacts have been found in inland Syria and in the Negev, but whether they had the same homeland as Abraham is impossible to say. It certainly seems highly unlikely that their culture represents the immediate background from which the Patriarch came or that Abraham is to be dated to this period. However, after a thousand years a considerable new element was added to the population of Palestine. The duration of this period is uncertain, and the period is indicated by various names by different excavators. (Chaliciform culture, M.B.I. etc.)

The Middle Bronze Age

It is estimated that domination by the nomadic element lasted from two to four hundred years. In the 20th century B.C. a new element can gradually be traced through archaeology. There is again a complete break in the pottery, and the nomadic groups, who may have become small farmers by this time seem to have had no influence on the newcomers. Like their predecessors they came from the north, this time however from or along the coast of Syria (Phoenicia). The route along which they came can be traced by comparison of the new pottery forms with finds at Byblos.

Once more the appearance of the country changed. The new pottery shapes point to a highly skilled craftsmanship of the potter. The mixing of the clay, the use of the fast-turning wheel, the elegant shapes of the pots, the finish with very regular and glossy burnish,

---

[1]) Kenyon, *Jericho* I, Ch. 5.
[2]) Kenyon, *Archaeology*, Ch. 6.

and the firing of the pots point to a strongly established tradition. Gradually town life appears again, often at the sites of the ruined E.B. cities. This culture can be said to have lasted right through the Middle and Late Bronze Age, until about 1200 B.C., and in many respects much longer. Until then the population remained virtually

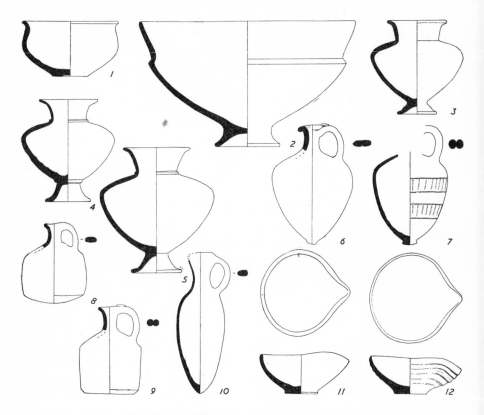

Fig. 16.   Middle Bronze Age pottery forms.

the same, and influences from abroad did not create the sort of new situation which can be discovered by archaeology.

A new period is inaugurated in the 12th century, first by the coming of the Philistines and related peoples, and somewhat later, when the Israelites become a real power in the country, a new culture made itself felt.

The period of approximately 7 centuries is divided into two subdivisions; the Middle Bronze Age and the Late Bronze Age. In the next chapter the Late Bronze Age will be dealt with. The cultural peak of the whole period falls in the M.B.A.

The M.B.A. becomes increasingly important for the study of the early chapters of the history of Israel. Many non-biblical texts have been found in surrounding lands, revealing much about ethnic movements in the Near East. It seems clear that especially in the case of their early law codices the Israelites had many early contacts with the kingdoms of northern Syria and Mesopotamia. There is a strong possibility that the background of the stories of the patriarchs is to be placed in the M.B.A. of Palestine. Thus both from the point of view of literary and purely archaeological evidence, that chapter of Palestinian archaeology which is our main subject ought to start with this age, almost a millennium before a true Israelite culture in Palestine came into its own.

The M.B.A. saw one spectacular event: the conquering of northern Egypt by the so-called Hyksos, who came through Palestine on their way south. The Hyksos have left some impressive remains in Palestine, but it is only from records, found in Egypt, that archaeology can 'label' those remains as Hyksos. From Palestine itself no written records of this time have survived. Yet our knowledge of the material remains, defences of the towns, house plans, furniture, industries, trade relations and burial customs is better than that of many other periods.

This is due first of all to the fact that it was a flourishing age in Palestine, prosperous within the limited possibilities of a country which both geographically and temperamentally tended against the formation of a strong unity. Unlike the two great alluvial river valleys where the success of irrigation and control over spring flooding depended entirely on a strong central government independent from local interests, the Palestinian landscape like Greece, definitely tends to separate its inhabitants. The new settlers of the M.B.A. did not greatly suffer from raids and especially after the Hyksos built their new type of defences, nomads were certainly no longer able to cause such havoc. The well-built town walls with battered glacis prevented the remains of the towns from annihilation in later times through erosion.

The best work on this period has been done by the last expedition at Tell es-Sultan under conditions highly favourable to exact archaeological results [1]). Jericho has yielded more information on this

---

[1]) K. M. Kenyon, *Digging up Jericho*, London, 1957.

period than any other Palestinian site up till now, and moreover the excavations at Jericho were the first to be executed in Palestine according to up-to-date standards of digging. Thus Jericho has become the key-site for the student of 'biblical archaeology' as far as the M.B.A. is concerned. Redating of the M.B. levels of sites excavated before the war can be done from the study of the excavation reports, now in the progress of publication.

At Tell es-Sultan more information about the life of the inhabitants was derived from the tombs than from the tell. Houses were preserved only in a limited area near the spring. The defences however could be studied in full. Owing to the special geological conditions of the Jordan valley many objects of perishable material (such as wood, leather, vegetable matter etc.) were preserved in the tombs which would otherwise have been completely lost, either in the destruction of the towns, or in the damp soil of the tombs.

Fairly soon after the M.B.A. began the country was invaded by the Hyksos. The name is an Egyptian ethnic word for Asiatics. They did not come as a wave of immigrants, but rather as a band or bands of warriors, who became the ruling class in the conquered countries. Unlike other invaders, they did not essentially influence the local cultures. In Palestine they may well have created favourable (peaceful) conditions for the development of the indigenous culture. They certainly promoted Egyptian influence in Palestine. From their capital in the Delta, Tell el-Yehudiyeh, they organised the defence of their kingdom in Palestine. A new type of defence was created, generally thought to be based on their own experience of capturing cities with a mobile army. Remains of this type of defence have been found at Tell el-Yehudiyeh, and in Palestine at Lachish, Jericho, Gaza, Fara, Hazor, and in Syria.

So little is known about the question of how the Hyksos succeded in capturing Egypt after their long journey from northern Syria (?), that the purpose of the elaborate defence works is not yet quite clear. Basically the defence consisted of a high bank, in the shape of a modern sea-dyke, crowned with the town wall. The slope of the bank was made inaccessible at Jericho by cutting off the lower part of the slope, and strengthening the cut by a high retaining wall [1]).

It has been suggested, that the system was designed to resist surprise attacks by an army that used chariots and was able to move

---

[1]) Kenyon, *Jericho* I. Ch. IX.

quickly from one point of attack to another. Another explanation is that the defenders found a high place and free field in front of them to use the arrow, whereas it is also suggested that primarily the defences were meant to make using a battering ram impossible. Archaeologically speaking there is an argument against all these theories: no remains of battering rams or chariots have ever been found in relation with the Hyksos in Palestine and it is extremely doubtful whether the armies of those days had archers, since no arrowheads have been found in undoubtedly M.B.A. context. This shows that archaeological evidence strictly used often leaves us in doubt. It is for instance clear that a battering ram could never be operated against a wall which was standing on a steep and slippery slope but the fact that no battering rams have been found is no proof against their existance in the time of the Hyksos. A better argument against this theory is, in the case of Jericho, that the walls anyway would have been erected on the edge of a fairly high mound with steep slopes as was the case with all the cities built either on tells or on natural hills. One of the purposes of this construction however may have been to prevent any attacker from setting the city on fire. Jericho has shown that such was the practise of the invading 'Amorites'. The new design would make this virtually impossible.

The rule of the Hyksos over Palestine came to an end, when the Egyptian Pharaoh made Egypt free from foreign domination. The fall of the Hyksos marks the end of the M.B.A. Probably the most important result of this liberation was that Palestine once more became a disconnected group of city states. The lack of unity makes itself felt in the following era by a gradual decline in the art and technique of local crafts.

As has already been said, the M.B.A. is the first period in which we can expect direct relations with the early history of the 'proto-Israelite' tribes. However, as long as no texts are found to relate events to the excavated ruins, archaeology cannot do any more than occasionally illustrate a background which may, or may not have some connection with Biblical narratives.

CHAPTER FOUR

CANAANITES, ISRAELITES AND PHILISTINES

The study of the Middle Bronze Age cannot be dealt with within the scope of this book [1]). In this chapter the situation in Palestine which can be concluded from the archaeological evidence concerning mainly the 13th, 12th and 11th centuries B.C. is discussed. This is a period in which the Canaanite culture declined and did not recover until two new groups, the Israelites and the Philistines had gained control over the country. Archaeologically speaking the Philistines should be mentioned before the Israelites as it is impossible to speak of an Israelite culture until after king David practically wiped out the Philistines as a cultural factor in Palestine [2]).

Palestine in the Late Bronze Age occasionally enters the limelight of historical documents. The main sources of information have been found in Egypt. Archaeologically important are the records of invasions of Egyptian armies by which the rulers of the xviiith and xixth dynasties maintained or restored their control over the important trade routes through Palestine or defended their country against invading nomads or displaced groups. Shortly after 1600 B.C. the Hyksos were expelled from Egypt and were most likely deprived of their power in Palestine. They may have formed an additional element in the Canaanite population, but lost their stimulating influence in cultural matters.

Once the Hyksos power and the political unity it had created was dissipated, Palestine again became a conglomeration of city states. From the archaeological evidence one can only deduce that a situation emerged in which inter-urban rivalry did more and more damage to the general prosperity. Egypt which naturally did not favour the rise of a united nation at its north-eastern border seems to have been

---

[1]) Consise treatment of this period is found in Kenyon: *Jericho* I, and *The Archaeology in the Holy Land*. For the pottery see *i.a.* A. Dajani: *Middle Bronze Age Pottery*, *A.D.A.J.*, Vols IV-V, pp. 99ff.

[2]) For this reason the new proposal by R. Amiram and Aharoni in *I.E.J.*, Vol. 8, pp. 171ff., to call the 12th and 11th cent. B.C. Israel I cannot be accepted. A) the territory inhabited by the Israelites before the time of the United Kingdom was only a small portion of the country, B) there is no question of the rise of a new culture for which the Israelites can be made responsible in these centuries.

content with a loose suzereinity in which local princes were allowed a good deal of freedom and even action against each other as long as Egypt profited from the trade routes and from Palestinian export goods.

As soon as, archaeologically speaking, the main characteristics of the L.B.A. were fully developed, Thotmes III invaded Palestine and captured Megiddo in 1479 B.C. It is thought that Megiddo Str. IX was destroyed in this action.

Soon other elements contributed to the general decay. In the second part of the L.B.A. wandering groups tried to settle in Palestine. Evidence for events mentioned in the Bible has not come from any archaeological site. In particular the destruction of no single town can be confidently attributed to any one of these invaders. There was, however, during the 14th century B.C. a correspondence between the local Palestinian princes and the Egyptian court at tell el-Amarna, where a large number of clay tablets were found. In these letters Egyptian aid is constantly being begged for against the intruding elements, and here the name Habiru appears, often thought to be philologically connected with the name of the Hebrews. The equation with Israelites remains difficult, since Habiru (Eg. 'Apiru) does not indicate an ethnic group although the Israelites may have adopted this name, indicating 'the ones that crossed' i.e. the river. Mercenaries, warrior bands, groups of slaves and displaced persons are all included in the word Habiru. This gives us a perfect opportunity to illustrate what has been said in the introduction. From literary sources dating from the period itself, i. e. the Amarna tablets, we know that certain groups of wandering people mentioned by name, tried to invade Palestine in order to settle themselves among the Canaanites. They also appear to have been powerful enough to cause much trouble to the local chiefs and although this is not clear, some may in fact have succeded in establishing themselves firmly, either by the force of arms, or by treaties with towns. In the Biblical narratives of the Israelite invasion which show at least a partial similarity to these events, their historical contemporanity is in fact far from certain. This point has been exhaustively discussed [1] and has brought about various interpretations of the biblical narratives.

On the other hand, apart from the archaeological discovery of the Amarna texts in Egypt that give us some historical information

---

[1] cf. Rowley, *o.c.*

about the situation in Palestine in that particular age, archaeology has as yet practically nothing to contribute to the discussion. Archaeology has not yet been able to discover in the material remains in Palestine any trace of the Habiru group mentioned in the Amarna letters. In cases where the archaeological finds seem to indicate foreign, non-Egyptian elements like the community that built and used the so-called Fosse Temple at Lachish, there are no means of connecting them with the literary evidence. As yet the bulk of the material remains from the L.B.A. in Palestine is still unexcavated, and much light will eventually be available once some L.B. sites have been properly examined. It is not impossible that as the Amarna letters were written in Palestine on clay, collections of cuneiform tablets might be found in those levels. Other useful information concerning the immigrating groups might come from imported objects which the families brought with them from their homeland, if they were buried with their dead in L.B. tombs or graves. This only shows that eventually archaeology may contribute some facts to what is known already and even may in certain cases give decisive proof one way or the other about the identity of the Habiru. However it would be entirely mistaken in the present situation to use archaeological evidence as proof in historical reconstructions [1]).

Apart from the people mentioned in the Amarna correspondence, other groups were on the move in the second half of the Late Bronze Age: presumably there were the early Hittites who settled in Palestine. Historically speaking their presence in Palestine cannot yet be explained satisfactorily [2]).

An event of major importance was the Palestinian action by Seti I (1320-1301), who firmly re-established Egyptian control over the country. For this event archaeology gives direct evidence. Excavations at Beth Shan [3]) brought to light a temple in which was found a stele commemorating the defeat of marauding bands which were attacking Beth Shan and other places from across the Jordan. The stele dates from the first year of Seti's reign. Beth Shan had henceforth an Egyptian garrison. Many objects are found both there and elsewhere which are imported from Egypt or locally imitated from imported wares. This restoration of Egyptian power in Palestine however did not promote the prosperity of the country. Palestine

---

[1]) cf. 'Die archäologisch-historische Methode' in Eggers, o.c., pp. 134ff.
[2]) cf. O. R. Gurney, The Hittites, Pelican Books no. A 259, pp. 59ff.
[3]) cf. pp. 64 ff.

had suffered heavily from the lack of security in the previous period.

Evidence of the political uncertainties of the time is shown in the many destructions of Palestinian sites, as discovered by excavations:

Tell Beit Mirsim Str. C. was destroyed about 1350 B.C.

Bethel Str. I by the end of the 14th century.

Megiddo Str. VIII in the middle of the 14th century.

The temple at Beth Shan Str. IX about the same time. Very little is yet known about the city itself.

Jericho had a short lived occupation in the 14th century which ended in the second half of it.

The increasing amount of barbarianism in this age may in some cases account for wholly or partly destroyed towns. However the L.B.A. is not only a time of violent disruptions. In the second half of the 16th century a new type of decoration appears in indigenous pottery, known as "bichrome wares". (fig. 17). It has been found in great quantities in southern Palestine but similar or related types have been discovered as far north as Ras Shamra on the Syrian coast and on Cyprus. Here again it is still difficult to detect where exactly this pottery originates, but it is likely that it is of Canaanite origin. The decoration is painted in black and red, and consists of metopes or crossed bands forming fields in which are drawn various geometric patterns and animals, oxen, birds, fishes and sometimes other animals.

This art of the potter's workshop flourished during the firm government of the early XVIIIth dynasty in Egypt. Soon afterwards the products of the Mycenean world entered Syria and Palestine, mainly produced in Cyprus and Rhodes and probably later also along the northern Syrian coast. This pottery is completely different from the local Palestinian wares in ware and technique, but it became increasingly popular and was often imitated by Palestinian potters. (Fig. 23). Thus there was a flourishing trade along the coast and across the sea with Cyprus. Tell Abu Hawam [1]) one of the few harbours along the Palestinian coast, was founded for this trade about 1400 B.C. The latest stratum (Str. V.) was destroyed according to the excavator c. 1230 B.C. at the end of the L.B.A. Thus preceding the violent penetrations from the east there was a peaceful infiltration of cultivated elements from the north-west. Pottery from Mycenean and Cypriot origin has been found as far east as 'Amman in (Trans-) Jordan.

---

[1]) *Q.D.A.P.* Vol. IV, nos. 1 and 2. 1934.

Fig. 17.   Decoration details from pottery from Stratum IX, Megiddo.

There are however no indications in the archaeological evidence that the population changed a great deal. From the 20th century there was a Canaanite culture in Palestine and this culture remained virtually Canaanite until the end of the L.B.A. This is most clearly indicated by the pottery traditions. Although obviously different from the true M.B. pottery, the pottery from the L.B. is developed

out of the M.B. shapes and techniques without any significant inter-
ruption, and apart from the painted wares (Bichrome and later
decorative art) the most characteristic feature in this respect is the
slow degeneration both of forms and of execution. This reflects the
decreasing welfare of the population as a whole.

A very slow recovery from this dark period must have begun soon
after the Israelites had established themselves firmly in the country.
How long a period it took to settle in the country we are still unable
to say. The archaeological evidence makes it clear that there is no
sudden change in the material culture by the end of the L.B.A.
The change over to a distinctly new culture is in fact much slower
than the rise of the Canaanite culture at the beginning of the M.B.A.
Archaeological evidence may point to the presence of Israelites in
Palestine in the 12th century B.C. but this interpretation is only
possible in the light of discoveries concerning later developments
and of biblical evidence. In the 12th century we find tentative beginnings of new pottery shapes and the negative evidence of a further
decrease in the skill of the craftsmen.

Thus there is a striking contrast between the well-constructed
Canaanite houses that were destroyed at Bethel at the end of L.B.
and the dwellings that replaced them in the 12th century. This could
be taken as a sign of a new population at the site [1]). While probably
coming from the eastern and southern borderlands and leading a
nomadic life, the Israelites cannot be expected to have had much to
offer to renew the culture of Canaan right from the start. Instead
archaeology has to search for signs of their military actions shown
in destructions of towns, and for new settlements [2]). A usually better
source of information is yet unsufficiently available, namely the
graves of the new settlers, that can be expected to be quite different
from those of the Canaanite population, especially in the earliest
stages.

Although the Israelites entered the country before the arrival of
the Philistines, it is the Philistines who first make their presence felt
archaeologically. They bring with them all that is required to provide
evidence of a new group. The Philistines, who arrived at the beginning
of the 12th century B.C., introduced a type of decoration in pottery
which they brought from their homeland. The introduction of iron

---

[1]) cf. Albright, *Archaeology*, Ch. VI.
[2]) cf. Y. Aharoni, *Problems of the Israelite Conquest in the Light of Archaeological
Discoveries*, Antiquity and Survival VI. II, 2-3, 1957, pp. 131ff.

as a metal which in the course of time replaced bronze is connected with them and they practised, at least partly, burial customs which were unknown to the Canaanites. Without the biblical evidence concerning the Philistines and the Egyptian records found at Medinet Habu archaeology would still have been able to state that a new group had settled early in the 12th century along the southern coast of Palestine, and that this group had left its northern (Aegean) home-land shortly before the end of the 13th century. Thanks to the historical texts mentioned above, the interpretation of the archaeological evidence is much clearer. The story of their coming from the Aegean world by land and sea, their attacks on Egypt and final settlement along the eastern Mediteranean coast is known from the Egyptian records. The Bible mentions the towns they occupied and their endeavour to conquer Palestine, as well as their final defeat [1]).

The second part of this chapter is arranged in the same way as the three following chapters. Four selected subjects are dealt with that are related with the late Canaanite period and the transition to the Iron Age and the culture of the Israelites.

1. A short description is given of Megiddo Level VII, A and VII, B. Megiddo at that time was a comparatively flourishing Canaanite town which was not immediately taken over by the Israelites (cf. Jos. xvii 11).

2. For its immediate evidence of Egyptian and other foreign influence in the country a description is given of a temple, found at Beth Shan level VII.

3. Amongst the first traces of the Philistines found in Palestine were tombs discovered by F. Petrie at tell Fara. One of those tombs is discussed here.

4. Jericho plays an important role in the narratives of the conquest of Palestine by Joshua. The archaeological situation at tell es-Sultan is described here as a good example of the limitations of archaeological evidence in connection with the Bible.

Megiddo, Stratum VII A and B.

Literature:

Megiddo II; Seasons of 1935-39. (1 vol. text, 1 plates), G. Loud, 1948, O.I.P. LXII, University of Chicago Press.

---

[1]) T. Dothan, *Archaeological Reflections on the Philistine Problem*, Antiquity and Survival Vol. II 2-3-pp. 121ff.

G. M. Shipton, *The Pottery of Megiddo Strata VI to XX*. S.A.O.C. 17. University
of Chicago Press.

A. Alt. *Megiddo im Uebergang vom Kanaanäischen zum Israelitischem Zeitalter*. Kleine
Schriften 1953.

On the date see Albright, *B.A.S.O.R.* nos 62, 68 and 74.

The Late Bronze Age city, Stratum VIII, was destroyed about
1350 B.C. and soon after that it was rebuilt following the same general
pattern, that is to say the previously existing buildings were restored
again.

Originally it had been the plan of the excavators of Megiddo to
strip the site completely from the top levels down to the lowest
remains, but this soon proved to be impossible, and excavation had
to be limited to certain areas. Thus a part of Stratum VII was excavated
in area AA and BB. This stratum lasted for about two centuries,
with one destruction which divides it in two periods, VII B preceding
VII A. Megiddo remained in this period a Canaanite town, long after
the Israelites occupied the hill-country.

Here it is only our purpose to describe in short a prosperous Late
Bronze Age II city so we need not trace the history of its buildings
back into their original layout in the Middle Bronze Age.

The plans of Str. VII B and A are given on pp. 60-63, figs. 18/19-
20/21. In VII A (area AA) the gate and a public building or palace
were found. This gate was built according to a well-known M.B.A.
type, found also at other sites such as Shechem and Tell Beit Mirsim.
The rise of the general levels of the city, caused by destructions and
rebuildings, and winter rains, which brought the mud from roofs
and walls into the streets, made it necessary to heighten the level of
the entrance of the gate. This gate had a long history of destructions
and rebuildings, additions, etc. Its layout is clear from the plan.
There is a long passage, divided by three pairs of buttresses. Although
nothing was found which makes the reconstruction of the higher
parts possible, it is fairly certain that there was a roof over the passage.

Southwest of the gate a substantial building, dating from Stratum
X was rebuilt, with the earlier plan still recognisable, although it
also underwent many changes in the successive periods. There was a
wide courtyard with rooms along the north and west side, and a
buttressed wall all along the north side. This may well have been the
palace of the local prince. In VII B it had in the north-west corner a
room with a raised floor and four steps leading into it, which was
possibly a private shrine. Since most of the floor had disappeared by
the reconstruction in VII A the contents had also disappeared, and

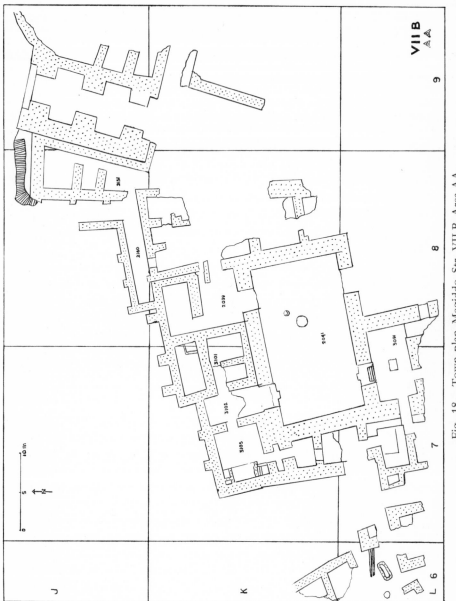

Fig. 18. Town plan Megiddo Str. VII B Area AA.

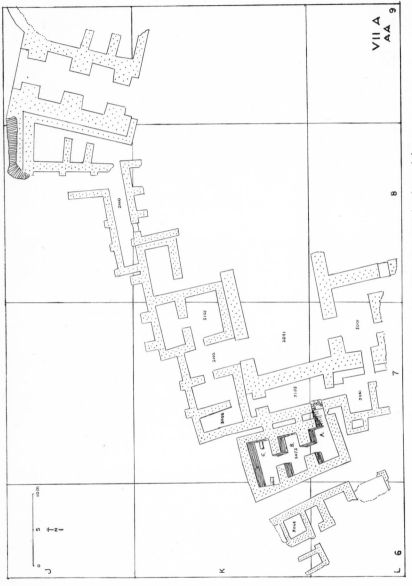

Fig. 19. Town plan Megiddo Str. VII A. Area AA.

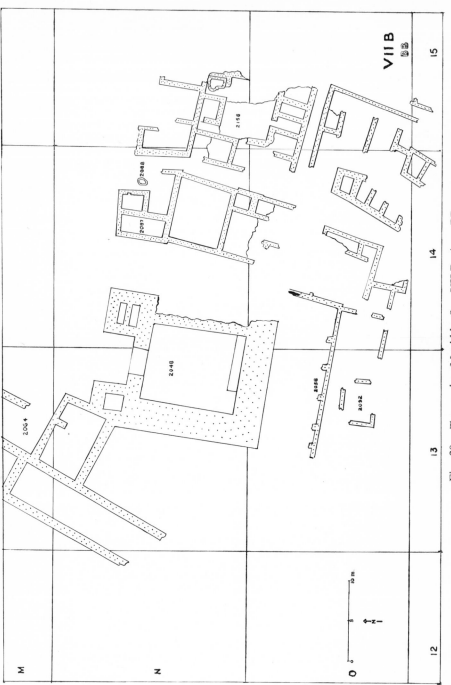

Fig. 20. Town plan Megiddo Str. VII B. Area BB.

so there is no material evidence and will not be until and if a similar
situation is found elsewhere with more certain indications.

In area BB we find once more that the layout of Str. X still existed.
Here we find the houses of the civilians and probably this was a
wealthy quarter. Although the plan is less clear than that of Str. X
we can see that the street and the four houses still exist, with the
original plan of a courtyard with rooms on three sides. The large

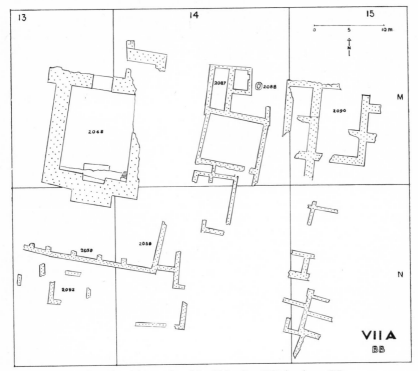

Fig. 21.   Town plan Megiddo Str. VII.A. Area BB.

building with heavy walls, which possibly was a temple and was
erected (according to the evidence available) in the previous stratum,
has an exact parallel in a building excavated by E. Sellin at Shechem,
the original date of which is even more uncertain. Two towers stood
in front of the building and guarded the entrance, which led into one
single room. The heavy walls may well indicate that this was a
building of several stories. According to Sellin the building at tell
Balata (Shechem) had been robbed of its contents before it was
destroyed in antiquity. Sellin was led to the identification of the

building with a temple by his equation of it with the 'house of the Ba'al Berith', mentioned in the Bible [1]). Inside the building at Shechem four pillar bases were found. According to the plans, drawn of this building by Welter, the towers were not solid structures (as they appear on Sellin's plans) but built in exactly the same way as those of Megiddo. Whereas the orientation of the building at Megiddo is north—south, that of the building at tell Balata is east—west. In both cases the evidence, published by the original excavators of the buildings, would date them in the beginning of the L.B.A. Further excavation at Shechem by E. G. Wright may throw new light on the date and purpose of both structures [2]).

Stratum VII A shows a number of minor changes in the plans of the gate and buildings. One very interesting new addition to the palace is the cellar at the west side of the palace. One entered the cellar by a flight of stairs, and it was divided into three rooms, containing what was left after the looting of a treasure, collected over a long period of time by the owners of the building. The objects consisted of objets d'art, partly imported from Egypt, Cyprus and Phoenicia. There were alabaster vessels, golden objects, gold with faience inlay, and, most important of all, ivories, which apparently had been collected from discarded furniture, which once they adorned as inlay. (Plate VIII).

After this town fell in ruins it remained unoccupied for some time, until it was newly erected on a completely new layout in the days of king Solomon.

THE 'AMENOPHIS TEMPLE' AT BETH SHAN

Literature:

A. Rowe, *The four Canaanite Temples of Beth-shan*, Beth-shan II, 1940 (The temple and cult objects).
G. M. Fitsgerald, *Beth-shan* II ii, 1930. (The pottery).

The excavators dated the level (VII) in which this temple lies on the evidence of inscribed material found in it, from 1411 to 1314 B.C. This date has been re-assessed and corrected by G. E. Wright in an article in the American Journal of Archaeology 1941, p. 485f. It has been lowered to the now generally accepted date of 1300-1150 B.C.

Let us take a look at the evidence produced by the authors and

---

[1]) Cf. *Z.A.W.* 1926, p. 305.
[2]) Preliminary reports in B.A.S.O.R.

see whether, with the help of modern pottery knowledge we can assess which end of the timescale this temple should be assigned to. It must be explained that one of the main reasons for the excavators' original date of this temple, and hence of the level in which it was found, was based on the fact that certain objects bearing the name of Amenophis III were found under the steps leading to the altar room. The excavators were misled because at the time of excavation it was not recognised that objects such as seals, scarabs and amulets were of a religious and artistic value which helped preserve them and keep them in circulation generations after the date of manufacture. They seem to have been handed down as family heirlooms and often given to temples, where they were preserved as part of the temple treasure. On the occasion of a re-building or change in cult within a temple these small objects seem to have often got mislaid and were casually incorporated into the new fabric. Cf. the Fosse Temple at Lachish [1]).

Fig. 22 gives the plan of this temple and in figs. 23-24 some of the objects found in each room are re-assembled. (Clearly not all the pottery shapes found have been published). Only four major loci have been dealt with here: the upper altar room 1068, the court 1072, the anteroom 1086 and the room east of the ante-room 1085. The other numbered areas said to be connected with this level all lie outside the main temple walls and may or may not be totally dis-associated with that building.

Here follows the description of some archaeological features by the excavators:

Vol. II: 1 p. 7 'the bases of the walls are by no means all on one plane. The builders seem to have made no attempt to level the ground for the foundations before they commenced to erect the temple, but merely sunk them at different depths in the debris. Then, after the walls were finished, they made a hard clay floor, apparently 10 cms. thick, in the court, at such a height as to be just above or on a level with the highest wall-base. The floor was presumably more or less level but few traces of it were discovered..... . The upper altar room had been partially destroyed'.

Vol. II: 2 p. 1f: '...it has been one of our principal difficulties

---

[1]) O. Tufnell, C. H. Inge and L. Harding *Lachish* II: *The Fosse Temple*. London, 1940. (The Wellcome-Marston Archaeological Research Expedition to the Near East).

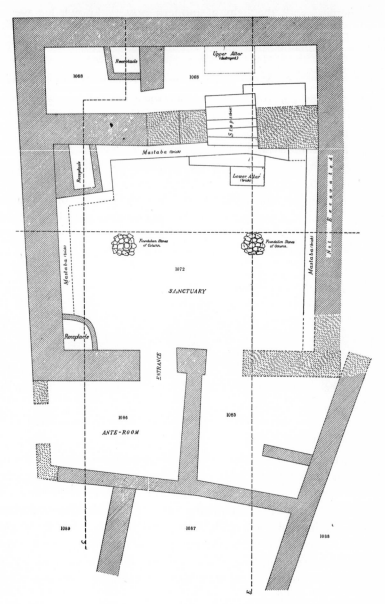

Fig. 22.   Ground plan of the temple of Amenophis III, Beth-Shan.

that the floor levels cannot as a rule be exactly determined. The floors were usually of hard clay, and the debris is so hard that the excavation often reached the stone foundations of unbaked brick walls without encountering any trace of a floor. *It must be admitted that occasionally objects work up or down from their proper level: thus three or four fragments from the Seti temple (immediately above) were found to fit onto pieces from the Ramesses or Amenophis level'.* (The italiecs are the authors).

With this due warning we read on the same page of Vol. II: 2, that the pre-Amenophis and Amenophis level 'include the floor level below the Amenophis temple, the level immediately under the temple floor, and that of the temple itself'.

The situation, however, is not as hopeless as it would seem. In the list of pottery in Vol. II: 2 and objects in Vol. II: 1 some finds are

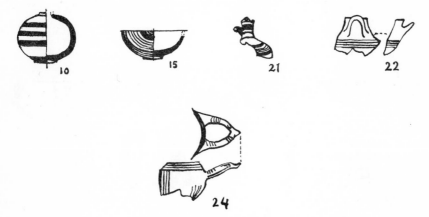

Fig. 23.   Imported pottery from the temple of Amenophis III.

said to come from 'below floor', 'below steps' or 'from a low level'. If we assemble these objects and divide them into foreign imports and local ware an interesting picture emerges. In fig. 23 dealing with room 1068 (the upper altar room) nos. 10, 15, 21, 22 and 24 are all foreign imports: possibly all from Cyprus.[1]) The first three date from Myc. III B, no. 22 probably from Myc. III C1. (These sherds are Mycenean in character but with comparison of forms seem more likely to have come from a Mycenean colony in Cyprus such as Engomi than the mainland itself) No. 24 is Cypriote White Slip II, and debased at that. Thus on the foreign imports alone the earliest part of this temple seems to have been in use in the end of the 13th

---

[1]) A large literature on the chronology of Mycenean and sub-Mycenean pottery exists. Among standard works are Furumark's *Chronology of Mycenean-Pottery*, Stockholm, 1941.

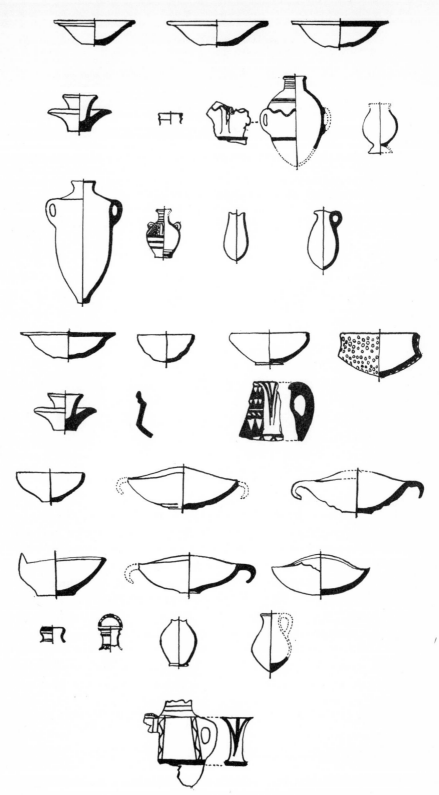

Fig. 24. Local pottery from the temple of Amenophis III.

century B.C. The indigenous Palestinian pottery, fig. 24, is all typically Late Bronze II—Early Iron Age.

As well as pottery, various extremely interesting objects were recovered in the temple. Some of these are assembled and drawn together in fig. 25. The bell shaped open cylinders with animal heads are unique and their use remains baffling. The rest of the finds reflect the complex international flavour of this cult: a lime stone altar hinting of Crete, an ivory castenet with Hathor head, Syro-Hittite

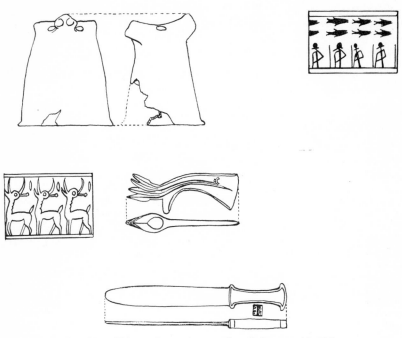

Fig. 25. Objects from the temple of Amenophis III.

cylinder seals, Egyptian amulets, a Hittite axe head, a Syrian dagger— the list piles up. Owing to the extremely disturbed nature of the temple which appears to have been plundered as well as burnt, it is very difficult to say what part these objects played in the cult. Very little was found in situ, only the pillar bases, a bin, a hearth and some offering benches.

What is even more interesting is that new temples were built on this site and in another part of the city, at a time late in the Israelite period. These bore a strictly non-Yahwistic nature. We know from inscriptions found at the site, that Beth Shan was first an Egyptian garrison city in the days of Pharaoh Seti I and that the Philistine troops, probably originally sent there by the Pharaoh remained its overlords until David's reign. There is no typical Philistinian pottery [1]) to suggest that these temples belonged to them, and indeed one was erected after the city came into Israelite hands.

PHILISTINE TOMB AT TELL FARA (NO. 552)

Literature:

Flinders Petrie, *Beth Pelet* Vol. II, p. 6ff.
T. Dothan, *Archaeological Reflections on the Philistine Problem*. Antiquity and Survival Vol. II (1957), p. 151ff.
K. M. Kenyon, *Archaeology* Ch. IX.

The content of this tomb group can be compared to and in some cases paralleled with four others at Fara itself, with anthropoid coffin

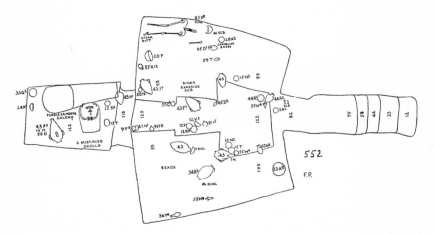

Fig. 26.   Ground plan of a Philistine tomb, No. 552, Beth-Pelet.

burials at Beth Shan and pottery from Tell Gemmeh, Gezer, Beth Shemesh, Askalon and Tell Beit Mirsim. All these sites have yielded examples of the very distinctive pottery known as Philistine.

Fig. 26 shows the plan of the tomb: a rock cut structure given access to by a flight of steps which led into a squared well with raised

---

[1]) The University of Pennsylvania Museum has announced that the yet unpublished finds from Beth Shan are in progress of being published. This of course may throw new light on the Philistinian occupation of the city. Cf. *Expedition* Vol. 3 no 2, pp. 31ff., 1961.

benches round the sides. On these benches lay the burials. Only one
other similar tomb at Fara contains an anthropoid coffin, Tomb 562.
The others have extended burials lying on their backs. This type of
burial is completely different from the normal Late Bronze Age—
Early Iron burials found in Palestine. The Canaanites of this period,
and apparently the Israelites too (on negative evidence) buried their
dead either in re-used M.B. shaft tombs or caves. These shaft tombs
were always roughly circular in shape, and without well or benches.
The dromos type of entrance to this tomb, which also occurs in the
others, hints at a foreign (Aegean) influence.

The pottery in this tomb includes much typical Palestine local ware
as well as the Philistine repertoire. The Philistine ceramic culture

Fig. 27.   Decoration details from a Philistine jug, Beth-Pelet.

seems to be an accumulation of forms and designs stemming from
the Aegean, particularly Rhodes and Cyprus, and Egypt. The decorative motifs are spirals, interlocking semi-circles, metopes with stylized
birds often pluming themselves, painted in red and black, fig. 27.
These motifs and the pottery shapes too seem to derive from Mycenean types from the end of the 13th century. The closest parallels
so far found come from Mycenean trading colonies in Rhodes and
Cyprus, particularly the city of Engomi, on the SE coast of Cyprus.
As Miss Kenyon points out (op. cit.) the vessels found in Palestine
are never exactly the same as their prototypes, even though they
combine the same elements. This suggests to her that the pottery
was made in Palestine in the outdated mode of the homeland of the
Peoples of the Sea, pottery which had been in fashion when they

left home at the end of the 13th century. Certainly the new contemporary 12th century Aegean types are not present and in no way influence these vessels. The Egyptian elements represented here by two jars with high, slightly bulging neck and two smaller handleless jars are both common types in Egypt and may have been brought by the Philistines or, seeing that we are dealing with a southern site not far from Egypt, these forms might have been introduced by Canaanite trade contemporaneously.

To sum up in the words of Miss Dothan (op. cit.) "We can assume that Philistine pottery is not a product of a people who came straight from their country of origin to the coast of Canaan and brought with them a homogeneous tradition. It rather reflects various cultural influences picked up on the long journey from the Aegean homeland. The mixture of cultural traits in this pottery is evidence of the disintegration of the Late Bronze Age culture out of which arose the new culture of the Early Iron Age".

This fits well with the literary evidence from the temple of Rameses III at Medinet Habu, which records the defeat of the People of the Sea in 1196 B.C. The record makes it clear that the defeated were a composite group of tribes, mentioning among others the Pulasti (Philistines) and Sherdanu (Shardans). "It is known on literary evidence that Shardan mercenaries were employed by the Egyptians and they are specifically mentioned as forming part of the Egyptian garrison in Palestine" as early as the Amarna period c. 1400 B.C., "..they may well have formed part of the group that settled in Palestine...while a related group may have formed part of the Egyptian garrison of Beth Shan" (Kenyon op. cit. p. 227).

In the tombs a number of bronze bowls were found as well as daggers and spears. There was one iron dagger with a bronze hilt and an iron knife. This is the first appearance of iron in a well dated context in Palestine.

The anthropoid coffin itself and the others found in Beth Shan are most interesting as they are completely new types of Palestinian artifacts with no indigenous ancestors or progeny. The coffin from this tomb group was cylinderical with a lid for the opening at the head. The lid bears a crude representation of a male human face, with distinctly bovine ears, with arms and hand encircling the face. The Beth Shan coffins also show the arms in this position, but the features are less debased. The Beth Shan faces are beardless and some wear what Miss Dothan suggests are stylized representations of the plumed head-dress shown on the Medinet Habu carvings.

Be that as it may, coffin burials of this type can be traced to Egypt with a 12th century group from Tell el-Yahudiyeh, offering good pottery parallels and both bearded and beardless faces on the coffin lids. Egyptian anthropoid coffins are found from the days of the Middle Kingdom till as late as 600 B.C., but are generally much superior in execution to these ones from Palestine.

The general distribution of this distinctive pottery fits with the territorial areas generally ascribed to the Philistines. This, with the exception of small amounts of sherd fragments which can be accounted for by trade, is largely confined to the coast. The influence of the Philistines spread inland and their suzerainity over the Israelites in the 11th century is proclaimed in the Bible but there is no question, archaeologically, of their settling in the central high lands. The one exception may be Beth Shemesh, where a great deal of Philistinian pottery was found, whereas Beth Shan has as far as is yet known [1] no Philistinian pottery, but had in fact, according to literary tradition a Philistinian garrison.

JERICHO

Literature:

K. M. Kenyon, *Digging up Jericho*, Ch. 11; London, 1957. id. *P.E.Q.* 1951.
J. Garstang and J. B. E. Garstang, *The Story of Jericho*, London, 193 .
E. Sellin and C. Watzinger, *Jericho*. Leipzig, 1913.

The Late Bronze Age at Jericho is discussed here as an excellent example of how earlier results of archaeological investigations can be corrected and of the problems which the archaeologist can sometimes present to Biblical scholars.

The only structural remains at tell es-Sultan found to belong to the L.B.A. by the latest expedition were a fragment of a house floor and an oven [2]. No evidence has been found of town walls or any substantial buildings, nor was there much stray pottery in the erosion levels belonging to the period. The L.B.A. pottery found by the earlier expedition [3] plus the recent evidence, dates the settlement to the first half of the 14th century B.C. The end falls between 1350 and 1325 B.C. The relevant material is reproduced here on fig. 29-30. This is taken from the above mentioned article by Miss Kenyon, in

---

[1] See note p. 56
[2] Garstang's 'Middle Building' and the supposed L.B. Palace are not discussed here, since they have no bearing on our subject.
[3] J. Garstang's reports in *A.A.A.*, 1930-1936.

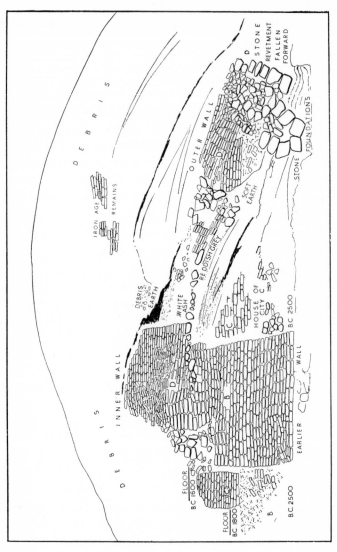

Fig. 28.   The fallen walls of City IV (from a measured drawing) B. Brickwall of
the Second City on the western scarp. DD. Walls of the Fourth City" Garstang
'The Story of Jericho', Pl. XVII.

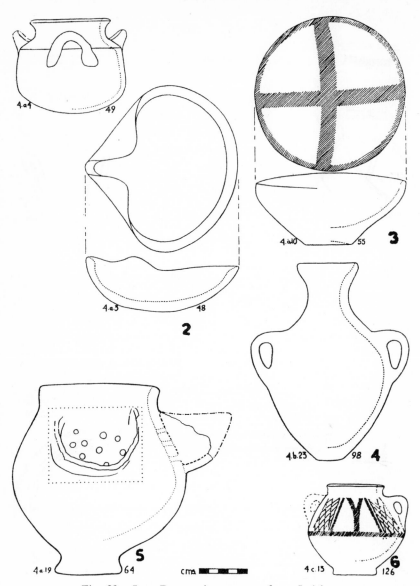

Fig. 29.   Late Bronze Age pottery from Jericho.

which the finds of Prof. J. Garstang concerning the Bronze Age are
discussed.

The reconstruction of the history of the fall of Jericho by Garstang
is shown in his section through the defences of the town at the north
side of the mound, fig. 28. The 'casemate wall' is marked D-D.

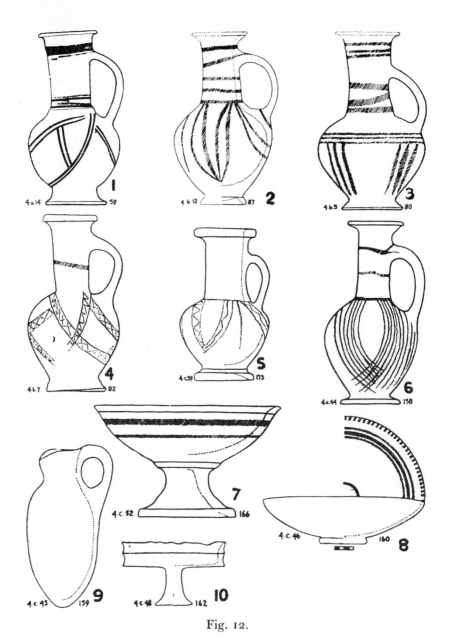

Fig. 12.

Fig. 30.   Late Bronze Age pottery from Jericho.

Fig. 6 shows a section from Miss Kenyon's excavation on the west side of the tell through the same defences, and from this it is clear that the so called 'casemate wall' precedes the great defence system, built by the Hyksos in the M.B.A., since it is buried underneath the fill of the first glacis. Moreover the double wall turns out to be two series of walls, the outer series of which was built after the inner series was long abandoned. Both series consist of a number of rebuildings and there is no question of any casemates. In fact the latest of these walls was destroyed a millennium before the coming of the Israelites, by the end of the E.B.A.

The date of the settlement of the L.B.A. was widely discussed after Garstang made his results known [1]. The comparative material, used by Miss Kenyon in her study for assessing the date is taken from

Megiddo Str. VIII, dated 1479-1350
Megiddo Str. VII, dated 1350-1170
Duweir Fosse Temple II, dated 1400-1325
Duweir Fosse Temple III, dated 1325-1230
Beth Shan Str. IX, dated 1400-1350.

In Kenyon, *Jericho III (the tell)* the matter will be discussed again and more recent comparative material will be included there. It seems likely however that the last expedition has uncovered practically all that remains of the L.B.A. on the tell and that no fresh material will be obtained from the site. Thus all the dating material is available and published. The following is not an attempt to give an exhaustive treatment of the subject, but sketches the outline of a renewed study of the archaeological evidence. Something will also have to be said about an approach along the lines of Biblical evidence.

Since Garstang's reconstruction of the fall of Jericho in the time of Joshua was based in fact on non-existant archaeological evidence, (evidence not related with the L.B.A.), we can only start from the latest results of the excavations. It seems clear then, that although Biblical scholars are inclined to pay attention exclusively to the date of the destruction of the town, there are more important questions to be dealt with.

There is no archaeological evidence that there was a walled town in the L.B.A. at Jericho. There is evidence that the site was inhabited

---

[1] Cf. Rowley, *o.c.*, pp. 12-16.

during a period of at the most 75 years. Just one house floor was all that remained in our days, and erosion had already begun to wash this floor away. There is very little L.B.A. pottery found in erosion levels at the site, and of over a thousand tombs not 1% can be attributed to the L.B.A. The short period of occupation and the evidence from the few tombs makes it clear that there never was a thick deposit of L.B. levels.

A serious problem, archaeologically speaking, are the town walls. Not only for the archaeologist, who finds no traces of L.B. defences but the construction of such walls must have been a tremendous problem to the settlers at the beginning of the 14th century B.C. Their predecessors had endeavoured to include the spring inside their huge defence system. Whereas the encircling bank, on which their wall was built, was thrown up on three sides against the existing tell, it had to be built up free standing from the lowest surrounding level on the east side in order to include the spring. From the plans published by Sellin and Watzinger it is clear, that the bank did in fact stretch out in the plain on the east side. The Hyksos must have solved the problem of the exit of water from the spring by constructing a tunnel under the bank. This, no doubt was the weakest spot in their defence system. If by falling debris from the wall above, the tunnel got blocked, the rising water would in a very short time undermine the bank. And the fact that the bank has disappeared completely on that side, (unlike the one at Hazor etc), may well indicate that this actually happened, either during a siege by the Egyptians or after the town fell in ruins. After the period of two centuries, in which the site lay unoccupied, this defect in the system must have come to light. Thus the new settlers had to face the question whether to include the spring and build a similar high bank and a wall on top of it and tunnel through it for the water or to leave the spring outside and return to the defence line of the early M.B.A. Besides, they had to deal with a completely derelict irrigation system, unless they were, what in fact our archaeological evidence suggests, people who settled in a oasis with very little possibility of building up a 'kingdom'. If they returned to the earliest M.B. system, excluding the spring from their town, the enclosed city would become much smaller and by analogy with so many other sites this wall would have given protection against erosion, which however has in the course of three and a half millennia almost completely removed the M.B. and the E.B. levels. This may well indicate that there was never a strong L.B. wall along the slope of the tell on the east side. In fact, nothing suggests the strong city, pictured in the book of Joshua.

These are some archaeological questions. The archaeological study of the L.B. 'city' at Jericho has to include the study of the destruction of the M.B. Hyksos city and the intermediate period as well. And this study is made necessary by the Biblical narative.

The Biblical evidence, on the other hand, has divided Biblical scholars into two main groups. Two widely differing theories concerning the date of the campaigns of Joshua have been constructed. Adding up the dates given in the O.T. may lead to the conclusion that Joshua functioned in the first quarter of the 14th century, whereas a critical study of the sources may bring the balance of opinion to the second half of the 13th century B.C. The descrepancy with the archaeological evidence is obvious in both cases. One aspect is once again closely related with archaeology. The Biblical narratives link the Jericho episode with the sojourn near Gilgal and with the fall of the city of Aï.

Gilgal then ought to be considered as a L.B.A. sanctuary, probably connected with a small settlement in an oasis. For centuries Gilgal has been 'identified' with various places round Jericho. In recent times more than one archaeologist has tried to find Gilgal, but no traces have been found yet [1]). Even if Gilgal was not an existing sanctuary before the coming of the Israelites, there ought to be the pottery dating from the end of the L.B.A. of which there are no traces near Jericho. (Tell es-Samrat is definitely of Herodian origin, the sites near Khirbet Mefjer are I.A. II, and the other known sites widely strewn around Jericho date from Byzantine times.) The conclusion is that Gilgal cannot yet help us to elucidate the Joshua period.

The case of Aï is worse. Excavations at the site have shown that this town was destroyed, like Jericho, at the end of the E.B.A., and not inhabited for about a thousand years, until long after the Israelites had entered the country [2]). After his excavation at Bethel, Albright suggested that, since this site is destroyed at the end of the L.B.A. but not mentioned in the Bible as a captured city, the story of the defeat of the people of Aï originally referred to Bethel. Since the excavation of Bethel still awaits its final publication, it remains to

---

[1]) J. Muilenburg, *The Site of Ancient Gilgal*, B.A.S.O.R. 140, 1955.
[2]) J. Marquet, *Les Fouilles de ʿAy (Et-Tell)*, Beyrouth, 1949.

be seen, whether the date of the destruction of the L.B. city of Bethel coïncides with the end of the L.B. settlement at Jericho [1]).

Biblical scholars, who are inclined to consider the Gilgal-Aï-Jericho cycle of stories as religious teaching dating from a later period, and based on popular explanations of the enormous ruins of the two destroyed cities,—Aï a vast heap of stone debris, and Jericho with the very high remains of the Hyksos defences,—will find that the archaeological evidence supports their interpretation, be it with negative evidence.

On the other hand however, Miss Kenyon has pointed out that only too often literary criticism has in the past denied historical values to old traditions (Troy, and in England the traditions about the King Arthur stories) and strongly favours the claim that the initial conquest of the country by Joshua as reported in the narratives contain historical data. If this is true, archaeologists can do no more than challenge Biblical scholars to re-examine their evidence.

A note on the miraculous elements in the old traditions: the archaeological evidence does not provide us with any indications that the end of the L.B. town of Jericho was brought about by unusual agents.

---

[1]) Albright, *Archaeology*, Ch. 5.

CHAPTER FIVE

ARCHITECTURAL REMAINS

In this and the following two chapters we turn to the study of some of the material remains of the culture of Israel in the Iron Age. From the study of these selected subjects a general picture emerges of how the Israelites lived, their towns and houses, their workshops and the products of their industries. The study of these subjects, as presented here, deals with excavation reports, and should enable the reader to continue his own explorations in those reports. For instance, from the study of the Iron Age defences of Lachish, the reader can turn to other reports for comparative material, like the walls of Megiddo, tell en-Nasbeh etc. It will be found then, that the gate of Megiddo is not like the one at Nasbeh or the one at tell Beit Mirsim. Archaeology finds general types, like the houses from tell el-Far'a discussed here below which are typically Israelite houses, whereas on the other hand each building and each object may show individual traits and tell its own story. Rather than listing all that has been uncovered by many excavations, some carefully chosen objects have been discussed here more thoroughly than otherwise would have been possible. In this chapter we deal with the architectural remains that can be found in an Israelite town: the wall, the gate, a palace, store house, fortress, civilian houses, waterworks. Apart from the fact, that these remains may vary from place to place, they may also have been different at different ages. Moreover, archaeology usually has to content itself with the fact that often little more than the ground plan has survived. The temple of Solomon is not included in this chapter, since its reconstruction is entirely based on literary evidence and comparative material from outside Israel. No traces of it have survived on the spot.

FORTRESS OF SAUL AT GIBEA

Literature:

A.A.S.O.R., Vol. IV, 1924. *Excavations and results at Tell el-Fûl* (Gibea of Saul) by W. F. Albright.

A.A.S.O.R., Vol. XXXIV, 1960. *An Archaeological Study of Gibea* (*Tell el-Fûl*) by Lawrence A. Sinclair.

The site was explored by Albright in 1922 and in 1933. After the first preliminary report, nothing else was forthcoming, until with his retirement from Johns Hopkins University pending, Professor Albright gave his excavation material and notes to promising students to publish for him 'under close supervision'. This turns out to be a very unsatisfactory situation for all concerned, and has resulted in the final publication, although brought out in 1960, conforming in almost every way to the standard of the publications of the '20s.

To illustrate this, and before we can turn to a study of the fortress itself, the criteria used for the dating of the building has to be considered. Some important deductions have been made concerning the typology and dating of the Early Iron Age in Palestine from the results of this dig. Now that the final publication is out, it is fair to say that some of the 'evidence' for pottery dating has vanished into thin air, and it is worthwhile looking into these misconceptions.

Connected to the remains at Tell el-Fûl is a type of jar, fig. 31 which Albright calls a 'fossil-type' or key type, as he takes it to be a sure indication of the first Israelite settlement in the country. Before examining the evidence for this 'fossil-type', it must be pointed out that three periods of occupation were found on the site, all on the highest part of the rock [1]). Below the fortress attributed to Saul was a Middle Bronze Age occupation without any structural remains, and a rock-cut installation with a wall, the latter being shown in Vol. IV, Pl. xxii, 'at the bottom of Room F', i.e. certainly not resting on a floor, but probably underneath and therefore without any archaeological relationship to that room.

Fig. 31 shows the jar rims published op.cit. Pl. 20. Here follows a list of their find spots:

No. 2 and 4 were found in debris outside the fortress to the north, No. 5 was found in debris outside the fortress to the east, no. 9 was in the fortress 'at the bottom of Room B' and no. 13 was in Room 10. Room 10 belongs to a Hellenistic house complex on the eastern edge of the hill. From "the bottom of room B' can be found anything dating from M.B. times and later, and in debris outside a wall nobody should look for dating evidence of that wall. The reader of Ch. II of this book will be able to see the falacy of making deductions on such flimsy evidence. This general lack of precision in corrolating finds and find spots makes it inadvisable to connect this building with historical data.

The published pottery, said to come from Fortress I and II, belongs

---

[1]) A.A.S.O.R., XXXIV, Pl. 27.

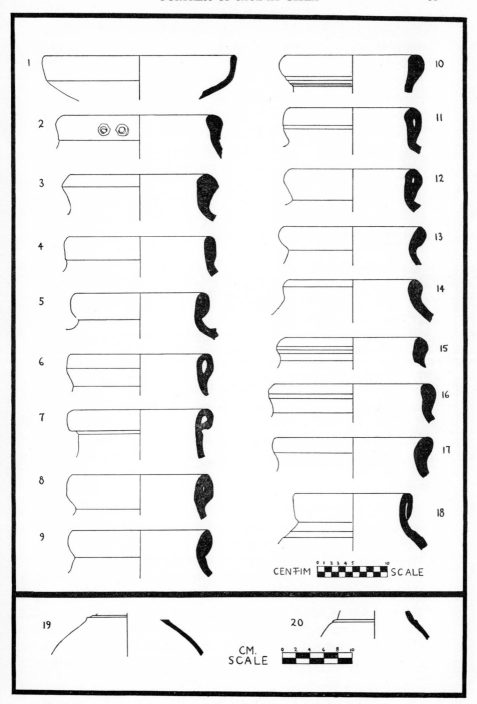

Fig. 31.   Iron Age rims from Tell el Fûl; the so-called Israelite 'fossil-type'.

to the Early Iron Age. It shows some typical features, of which the
burnishing technique is the most important. Sinclair lists the following
characteristics [1]:

Irregular hand burnishing on a dark red slip, covering the entire

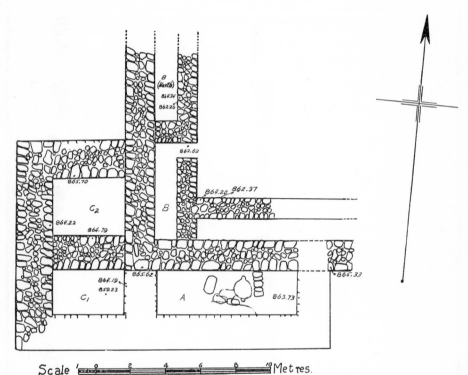

Fig. 32.   Plan of the Southwest corner and tower of Saul's fortress. Sinclair
'An Archaeological study of Gibeah, (Tell el Ful)' pl. 30.

outer surface. This type of decoration is frequently found in Palestine
before the end of the 10th century.

Irregular hand burnishing on the original surface of pots.

In some cases the hand burnishing has a criss-cross pattern of
lattice work.

No evidence of wheel-burnishing.

The fortress was rebuilt two times. It stood on the highest part of
a hill, where the natural rock crops out, and only part of it was preserved. This is mainly the sw corner (fig. 32) which was analysed as

[1] *O.c.*, p. 18.

follows. All the walls were built of large rubble masonry. There was an outer and an inner wall, respectively 2 m and 1.20 thick (according to the plan, whereas the writer notes 1.20 and 1 m. resp.) They are contemporary and thus formed a casemate wall with an over all width of 4 m. But from the plan we deduce that the outer wall was first built, since the transverse walls between the outer and the inner wall are not bonded into the outer wall. Similarly the tower, which was built against the corner on the outside was not bonded into the main wall. The thickness of the tower walls was over 2 m.

The excavators of this Gibea-fortress base their interpretation that the tower consisted of several stories on the fact that much burned timber was found inside the walls. Analysis of the wood has shown that cypress and pine wood were used for the wood construction, whereas in the third fortress or rebuilding almond was used. This would indicate a deforestation of the hills in the early days of the Kingdom. The amount of charred wood might well indicate that the superstructure of the tower was entirely made of wood.

Sinclair dates this first fortress ca. 1020-1000 B.C. One often finds the hypothetical reconstruction of the whole building reproduced in popular books about Palestinian archaeology, and it is considered to have been Saul's residence, be it a humble one. It is furthermore presumed that during the building of the 3rd fortress or tower most of the earlier building was cleared away down to bedrock.

The identification of tell el-Fûl with biblical Gibeah is generally accepted. In fact this is the only basis for the identification of the building and its history with the history of Saul and of the village[1]). It is by no means possible to accept as close a dating as Albright— Sinclair give on archaeological evidence. There is also no evidence that the 'fortress' was originally or later more than just a small stronghold which may or may not have been used by king Saul and his father as a palace. Every serious reconstruction has to be based on material evidence, and in this case it is lacking.

IRON AGE TOWN WALLS OF LACHISH

Literature:
Lachish III (Iron Age), Text and Plates, London, 1953. O. Tufnell.

Town walls have been found at various sites. Sometimes, as at

---

[1]) N.B. No remains of an early Iron Age village have been found at tell el-Fûl. The earliest remains of a village are Hellenistic according to Sinclair.

Tell en-Nasbeh the walls have been completely uncovered and traced round the city. It is impossible to conclude from the excavation report of Tell en-Nasbeh at which time the wall was built, although it seems certain that it is an Iron Age wall. Portions of I.A. walls have been uncovered for instance at Hazor, Megiddo, Gîb, Tell Beit Mirsim and Lachish. Though in fact little is known about the inner town wall at Lachish (Tell ed-Duweir), the finds from that excavation are described here, because a contemporary picture of the walls of Lachish has been found on bas-reliefs in the palace of Sennacherib at Nineveh [1].

The excavation of tell ed-Duweir by the Wellcome-Marston Archaeological Research Expedition to the Near East under the direction of J. Starkey [2] started in 1932 and was continued annually until the leader of the expedition was killed by brigands on the road in Palestine in 1936. Thus the excavation was never finished and inside the town only a few levels with some buildings have been examined. Much work was done on the gate of the town and the walls were traced and partly excavated. In a guardroom in the gate ostraca were found, consisting of letters written in the time of the Babylonian attack on Palestine [3].

The defences to be described here both belong to I.A. II (Albright's system cf. p. 36)

The latest wall belonging to the I.A. and likely to be the one destroyed by the Babylonians, was discovered in the area of the city gate, cf. fig. 33 (square F 16-19,4), and the section fig. 34. This wall was built on the stump of an earlier mud brick wall, which was 6 m. wide. The new wall was only 3.70 m wide, and was, as far as it was preserved, built of loose rubble and stones in the core, and a single row of stones as foundation. The inner and outer face of the wall were constructed of undressed stones only a single course wide on both sides. The outer face is vertical, whereas the inner face has a slight inclination. The lower courses of stones of the outer face showed traces of white plaster. Along the remaining section of the wall recessed panels, 14 m in length alternated with salients measuring 4 m. The original gateway in this wall was 4.40 wide. Some evidence

---

[1] Now in the British Museum.
[2] Published by Miss O. Tufnell. Op cit.
[3] H. Torczyner, *Lachish* I. 1938.
[4] *Lachish* III, Plates., Pl. 108 and Pl. 109.

for the date of construction comes from under the southern pier of this gate, where potsherds were found that can be associated with level III. Therefore this wall cannot be earlier than that period. Level III is dated c. 800-700 B.C., the last date being the year in which Lachish was beseiged by Sennacherib and destroyed. Miss Tufnell

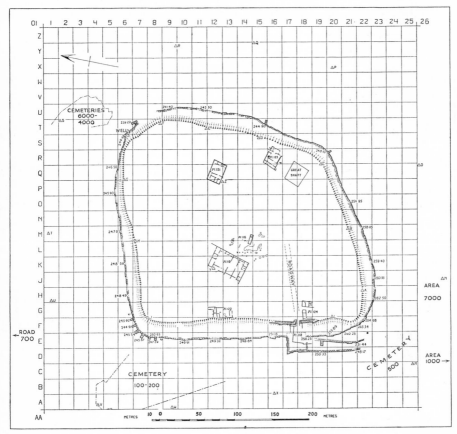

Fig. 33. Ground plan of Tell ed Duweir (Lachish).

identifies the 6 m. wall with the one pictured on the reliefs from Nineveh [1]) and the later wall must then be associated with the re-building of the town in the 7th century. Cf. *o.c.* the 'pictorial summary' on p. 102.

Of the 6 m wall only a small part was exposed. This is a wall built

---

[1]) *o.c.*, p. 60.

of mud-bricks, set in mud mortar, on a foundation of a single layer
of river stones. At one place the preserved height was 2.5 m. The
base of this wall was in places protected from erosion by a mass of
stone blocks set in mud mortar. This wall showed a style of recessing
similar to that of the revetment below. This and the revetment wall
are thought to be the walls pictured on the reliefs from Nineveh.

On the plan, fig. 33 the crest of the hill is indicated by a broken

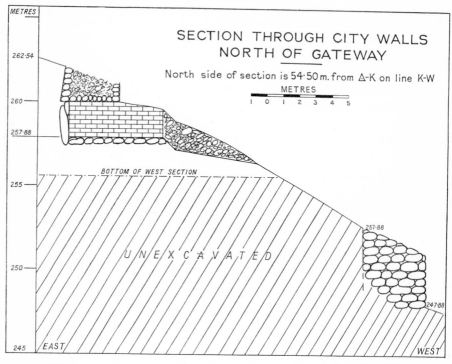

Fig. 34. Section through the Iron Age city walls of Iachich, 1936.

line. Outside this line is a steep drop almost everywhere [1]). It is quite
possible that this line indicates the course of the 6 m. wall, since
such a strong wall would certainly protect the edges of the crest
against erosion for a long time. Below the crest, on the slope a second
line is found on the plan, indicating the position of the revetment wall.
The outline of this wall was traced during the earlier seasons of the
excavation in order to define the limits of the area to be excavated.
This lower wall was built on the slope, and the foundation trench

---

[1]) *o.c.*, Plates, Pl. 106.

was cut through the wash from the tell down to the natural lime-stone rock. It was a revetment wall in so far as the inner face of the wall partly rested against the earlier erosion levels from the tell.

Evidence for the date of construction of this wall was found in a layer of compact marl, which was intentionally piled up against the foot of the wall and covered with a layer of red clay, which was brought up from the valley. The purpose of the clay-sealed marl was to prevent the soil at the foot of the wall from being washed away by rainwater, which would cause the collapse of the foundations. This means of protecting the wall must have been divised soon after the wall was built and thus belong to the same age. The compact marl however contained potsherds some of which dated from I.A.II, which is later than. c. 900 B.C.

The lower part of this wall is entirely stone-built. There are two different techniques practised here, which are thought to have been used simultaneously. The best constructed section of the wall consists of lines of large stones. At one place there were 11 courses of stones preserved to a height of 5.80 m. The face of this wall inclined at an angle of 20. Other sections however were built of smaller stones; they were higher and extended partly over the top of the adjoining sections, showing there the pattern of recessed panels. Between the sections built of smaller stones, and on top of the sections first described here were sections built of mud bricks. The whole upper part of the wall had been plastered with thick coats of lime plaster. It would seem that the less well built sections of smaller stones were repairs of the original wall, but the excavators concluded that these sections served to negotiate difficulties caused by the shape of the bedrock.

Everywhere, where the wall was excavated down to bedrock, traces of butresses were found at regular intervals, some projecting 4-5 m from the line of the wall, and there was evidence that the space between the butresses on the north side had been filled with stones and lime plaster to form a solid matrix.

Both position and height of the wall indicate that it was primarily a defence wall. At various places outside the wall were found the remains of towers. Two large breaches in this wall were found, where according to the situation and the arms found there, it was deduced that an enemy had forced his way through.

The Assyrian artist who carved the bas-relief at Nineveh, com-memorating the victory over Lachish by Sennacherib may have seen the city during the siege. If his work can be trusted we can get some idea of how the mud brick super-structure of the wall looked in reality. Even if he used his imagination there, many other details are faithfully depicted and worth studying.

TOWN PLAN AND HOUSES OF TELL BEIT MIRSIM STR. A

Literature:

The Excavation of Tell Beit Mirsim, Vol III. *The Iron Age*, by W. F. Albright. The Annual of the American Schools of Oriental Research. Vols. XXI-XXII. New Haven 1943.

The circumference of the Iron Age town walls of several Palestinian cities has been traced by excavations. There is evidence from various sites that in the Iron Age during the Kingdoms towns were rebuilt after a complete destruction according to the following plan. The wall was a proper casemate wall. On the inside against this wall one row of houses was built. At a distance of 15 to 20 m. from the wall there was a ring road, from which various roads led to the centre.

The plan fig. 35 shows the south-east corner of Stratum A at tell Beit Mirsim. This stratum [1]) represents the town which was built after the destruction of Str. B, probably caused by an attack of an Egyptian army under Pharaoh Shishak c. 918 B.C. This stratum lasted for more than three centuries until the final destruction by Nebucadnesar c. 589 B.C. The town walls of Str. B remained in use in Str. A. This was a double wall. The outer wall is 2 m. wide and the inner wall is slightly smaller. These walls were linked by cross walls at intervals. The existing remains were built of undressed stones. This type of casemate wall is found in many Iron Age sites. In Str. A the casemate rooms were used as store rooms, as was the case e.g. at Hazor. Two gates were found, each with a complicated history, one at the south east side and the other at the north west side. Cf. fig. 35.

The plan gives a good impression of the crowded houses between the ring road and the casemate wall, and some houses inside the circle of the ring road. In this corner there were no public buildings. The houses show basically one type. In a space, enclosed by four walls

---

[1]) This stratum was excavated between 1926 and 1933 by the Joint Expedition of the Pittsburgh-Xenia Theological Seminary and the American School of Oriental Research in Jerusalem under the direction of W. F. Albright.

with an entrance in one of the walls, there is a line of four or five stone pillars, slightly off centre. The excavator suggests that the pillars supported a roof over the smaller part, leaving the larger part as courtyard. The smaller part was often partitioned, whereas the larger part never was. A later development may be that the pillars were incorporated in a wall, closing the smaller part from the courtyard. At the end or alongside the courtyard there are one or two rooms. None of these rooms appears to have had any paving. In some cases a stone staircase was found outside the house, leading up to a flat roof or a second storey. Usually there were no traces of doors on the ground floor. The height of the ground floor could be measured from the remains of the staircases. The floor of the second storey or the roof was about 2 m above ground level. Albright concludes that the family worked downstairs and slept in a room or rooms upstairs. Lack of space may have forced families to use wooden ladders to go upstairs rather than staircases.

Evidence of industries was found in many cases. Albright suggests that the pillars were used to support upright looms In the houses were found many bins, stone bowls like mortars etc. but silos like those found in Str. B. did not occur in Str. A. An important industry was dyeing. (cf. p. 138).

The plan, shows many later additions to the original layout of the houses. Part of the circular street is shown and some sidestreets, either leading to the wall or to the centre of the town. The street level rose considerably during the three centuries of Str. A, and this fact alone made many adjustments necessary. It is also clear from the plan that lack of space became an increasing problem. The excavator states that outside the town wall at the south side a new quarter arose, so that many families lived outside the walls.

Evidence for flat roofs was found in the many cylindrical roof rollers, shaped out of stone boulders. There is sufficient proof from various excavations that roofs in the Iron Age were constructed in the same way as it is still done for cheap dwellings to-day. Wooden beams were laid at short distances from each other across the top of the walls and a layer of strong reeds, forming a basis for a thick level of clay were laid on top of them. The reed used for this purpose grows along the perennial streams. The clay was spread over the reed after mixing it with water and straw, as mud. Each year, in the dry season, the roof would dry out and crack at many places, and the first rain would pour through the holes. With the aid of a roof-roller the roof could be quickly mended, and if the rain had washed down too much mud, fresh clay had to be added. The roof would then be waterproof until the next wet season. The wearing down

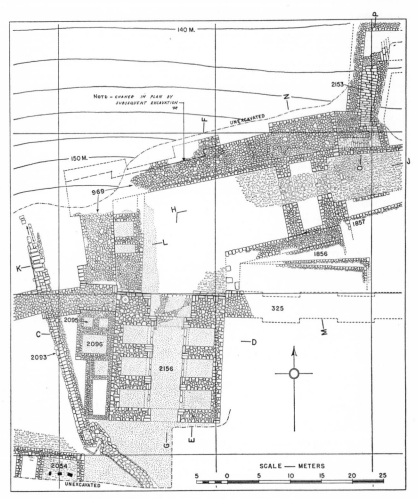

Fig. 36. Plan of the gate of Megiddo Stratum IV.

of the roof could be diminished by adding a layer of plaster, and there is proof that walls were treated in that way. However, every year a new level of mud would heighten the level of the streets. A stone pavement of cobbles would soon be covered under mud and disappear. This may indicate that in those cases where cobbled courtyards or walks are found, the roofs were better protected against wear from the rains. Various walls, shown on the plan, may have been adaptations to the risen street levels.

There seems to have been no drainage system in Str. A. Rainwater in the streets that could not escape through one of the two town gates, would sink into the tell.

The most flourishing time of Tell Beit Mirsim, according to the excavator, was the eighth century B.C. The maximum space inside the walls was ca. 3 ha. (7.5 acres) on which 150 to 250 houses could have been built, depending on the space that was taken up by public-buildings such as the local governor's house and store houses. The excavator estimates that the population was between 2000 and 3000, which is certainly not too high. Compare the plan o.c. Pl. 2 of Str. B.

The town must have suffered heavily from the Assyrian invasion under Sennacherib in 701 B.C.

THE STRATUM IV TOWN GATE OF MEGIDDO

Literature:

G. Loud. *Megiddo* II, Text. The Universtiy of Chicago Oriental Insti*t*ute Publications Vol. LXII 1942.

The gate was an important building in ancient walled cities. The entrance through the walls into the town was normally situated on the side where approach to the city was easy, *i.e.* where the slope of the hill on which the town was built was least steep. This would naturally also be the place where an enemy would try to break through the defences. The city gate had to be built in such a way that there was ample room for the defenders to manouevre when attacked. In peaceful times, the town guard was housed here. It performed rudimentary police duties, such as preventing criminals escaping out of the city. Partly because of their presence there, and partly because of the crowded conditions inside the walls, justice was dispenced there (cf. Ruth) and business deals clinched at the gate. The gate way or ways were also the main exits for drainage.

The shape and construction of the gates in the Iron Age was largely based on a long experience of enemy attacks and defence against them. The gate of Megiddo, attributed by the excavators to Str. IV, is called by Guy [1] 'unique'. However, during the excavations at Hazor [2], Y. Yadin found a gateway there that is exactly similar in

---

[1] *O.c.*, p. 47.
[2] To be published in *Hazor* III.

plan, and from this he concluded that a partly excavated building at Gezer [1]) could only be a similar gate. Since the Hazor gate was built in the 10th century, it is likely that it was built during the reign of Solomon, and the other two gates at Megiddo and Gezer, one would expect to be from the same architect.

Refering to the existing literature [2]), we confine ourselves here to a survey of the information given by the excavators of Megiddo and a discussion of the stratigraphy, based on their evidence.

These are the relevant facts as published in Megiddo II.

Str. V is dated by the excavators 1050-1000 B.C. (Early Iron II) Stratum IV is dated 1000-800 B.C., (Middle Iron). The gate of Str. V was only partially excavated, as the excavators wished to leave the Str. IV gate that was built on top of the remains of its predicessor, as a monument. No town walls existed that could be ascribed to Str V, and it was suggested that the back walls of the houses at the perimeter served as a wall. Yet the remains of the Str. V gate and its approach way were rather impressive. This approach way lies c. 2 m below the approachway of Str. IV gate near the entrance of the gate; that is to say, the pavements or made-up roads differ 2 m in height. This certainly does not mean that the fill between the two roads consists of one homogeneous fill of debris. The courtyard level of the Str. IV gate rose gradually, as the excavators observed from the position of a gutter running across it. And the approachway, being situated on a slope showed many signs of repairs and intermediate levels. (Cf. *o.c.* Fig. 106, sections H-J and M-N.)

According to the excavators, the superstructure of the Str. IV gate was entirely made of bricks, and only the foundations were of stone. These foundations reach the depth of 2.50 m. The faces of these foundations are only partly of roughly dressed stones; the inside faces of the piers and the corners are made of well dressed stones with straight margins, like the superstructures of other buildings of Str. IV. The profile of the upper course of stones shows that the superstructure was slightly recessed. There was a firm pavement, made of crushed limestone on that level, and the pavement between the piers was slightly higher. Inside the gate, the fill underneath this pavement is reported to have been an intentional fill, which would mean, that the whole area of the site of the gate was excavated before

[1]) *I.E.J.* Vol VIII, 1958. pp. 80-86.
[2]) See also Kenyon, *S.S.* III, pp. 201ff. and Crowfoot, *P.E.Q.* 1940, pp. 132ff.

the foundations were laid. Miss Kenyon [1]) has suggested that the type of stone masonry was not likely to be used for foundations, and also that the remains of the Str. V gate might well be in fact the original foundations of the Str. IV gate.

It is clear that the Megiddo publication does not provide us with conclusive proof for the attribution of the gate to Str. IV. Moreover there are some improbabilities: the Stratum V gate is said to be a substantial gate without a city wall. The other improbability is, that the stone 'foundation' of the Str. IV gate is exceptionally well made and must be regarded as monumental architecture which was meant to be seen and not buried under ground. The walls between the ends of the piers are not bonded into the 'foundation' but seem later additions. And finally the Str. IV town wall is not bonded into the Str. IV gate.

On the other hand, it seems certain, from the fact that the fill inside the gate was an intentional fill, that at one time the stone structure served as a foundation.

It is fairly certain that Megiddo Str. V was dated too early by the excavators. It existed between c. 1000 and c. 850 B.C. Str. IV is not earlier than the second half of the 9th century B.C. From the discussion of the stratigraphy of the gate it is clear that there is no stratigraphic evidence. On typological grounds, the masonry belongs to the period of the Omrids, Str. IV, but the plan may well be 10th century and Solomonic. Since both King Solomon and the Omrids employed Phoenician craftsmen to build in Palestine, it may well be that the style was introduced twice in the country but never taken over by the local craftsmen. In that case the gate in its original plan has to be attributed to Str. V, and the period of the second pavement, in which the masonry was buried, belongs to Str. IV. The Str. IV city wall is then a rebuilding of the original Str. V wall.

Fig. 36 shows the plan of the gate in Str. IV. The greater part of the gate is built inside the city wall, but the approachway is protected on the outside by a strong wall, guardrooms, and a smaller gate at some distance down the slope. An interesting feature is the flight of stairs, offering a short cut to pedestrians who went up or down along the slope. It seems that this passage was at least partly roofed. The main characteristics of the gate itself are the four piers on each side inside the gate. Traces of a door were only found between the front piers.

---

[1]) Kenyon, *Archaeology*, p. 248.

The Royal Quarter of Samaria

Literature:

G. A. Reisner, C. S. Fisher, D. G. Lyon, *Harvard Excavations at Samaria*, Cambridge, Mass. 1923.
J. W. Crowfoot, K. M. Kenyon, E. L. Sukenik, *Samaria-Sebaste* I. Palestine Exploration Fund 1942.
J. W. and G. M. Crowfoot, *S.S.* II, *Early Ivories from Samaria*. P.E.F. 1938.
J. W. Crowfoot, G. M. Crowfoot, K. M. Kenyon, *S.S.* III, *The Objects*. P.E.F. 1957.

Samaria was founded c. 880 B.C. by Omri, king of the northern tribes, who moved his capital from Tirza (identified by Père de Vaux with Tell el Far'ah, after excavations at that site from 1946 onwards; cf. p. 98) Part of the remains of Israelite Samaria were excavated by the Harvard expedition, 1908-1910 under the direction of Dr. G. Schumacher and Dr. G. A. Reisner with the assistance of Mr. C. S. Fisher, an architect. Work was continued in 1931 by a Joint Expedition under the direction of J. W. Crowfoot, and lasted for four seasons. The final publication (S.S.I) incorporates the plans of Israelite remains found by the earlier expedition as far as their identification seems acceptable.

Crowfoot, like Fisher before him, was an architect rather than an archaeologist. And the main excavation reflects this. But the stratigraphy of the site was taken care of by Miss Kenyon, who applied the archaeological methods in which she had been trained in England to a trench dug N-S right across the summit of the hill in the undisturbed area east of the Harvard excavation area.

The archaeological situation at Samaria is an extremely difficult one. Subsequent builders on the site dug down to bedrock to lay their foundations, destroying the earlier remains. Moreover building stone was taken from earlier buildings, including even foundation stones, to be fitted into later buildings. This explains why only small fragments of the earlier buildings were recovered. See the sections, S.S.I Pl. VII.

Miss Kenyon distinguished five building periods in the Israelite city, dating between the initial building of the town and its destruction by the Assyrians in 722 B.C. Fig. 37 shows the Israelite remains on the summit. Details on the west side are largely derived from the results of the Harvard expedition. On this hill Omri had the opportunity to build his court according to contemporary fashions in foreign lands. The palace area was surrounded by an enclosure wall, built of well-dressed stones and founded with one course of foundation

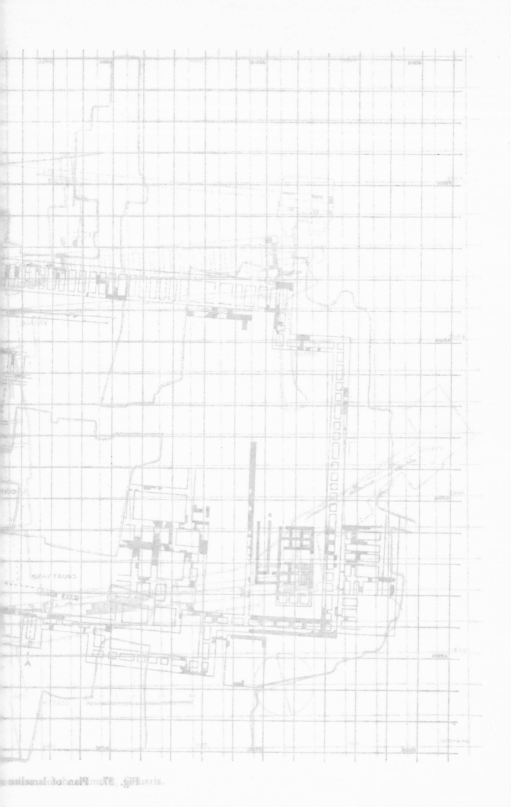

Fig. 37. — Plan of chamber tomb.

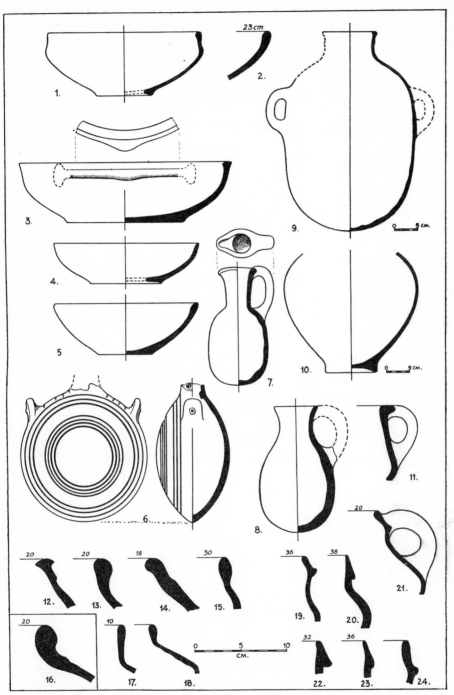

Fig. 38. Iron Age pottery forms, Samaria Period I.

stones on the rock. This plan was soon changed (in Period II) and outside and surrounding the enclosure wall a double wall, tied together by cross walls, was built thus forming casemates. Since this wall was built on the slope, the space between the first and the

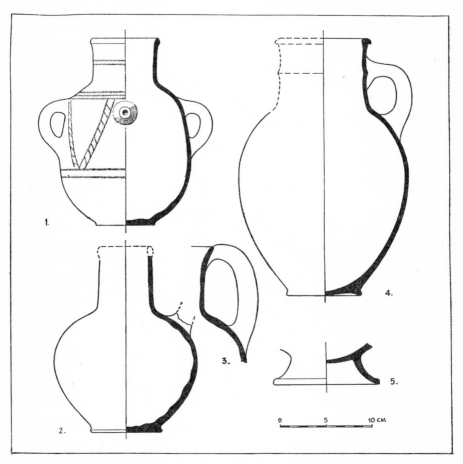

Fig. 39.   Iron Age pottery types, Samaria Period I and II.

second wall was filled with earth. So little remained of the earliest buildings inside the enclosure wall that no coherent plan of Omri's palace can be given. The entrance must have been on the east side where the rock does not fall away so steeply as on the other sides. Apart from the fine masonry from the first two periods, there are the remains of the ivories of Ahab's Palace to testify that within these walls once stood the Court of the Omrides Part of a courtyard was well preserved. It was well made and almost horizontal, and made of powdered lime. Apparently the buildings inside ran along the wall but at some distance from it.

Inspite of the apparently disappointing archaeological situation, owing to so much disturbance of the site, the information gained from this excavation is important, both historically and purely archaeologically.

Historically, it clearly shows us the position of the king in relation to his people in the days of Omri. The king lives apart from his people in a well-built citadel, behind very strong walls, in conditions where a despotic monarchy could flourish. The king was no longer chosen by the tribes as in the days of Saul. Omri, himself a usurper of the throne, knew the dangers that threatened his dynasty, not only from foreign powers like Damascus but also from court intrigues and ambitious military men. It also shows us that the king was no longer content to live a simple life as father of his people, but desired to bring his court in line with contemporary ruling powers, and live in some style and luxury, segregated from the mass of his people.

Archaeologically it is of importance because here at Samaria the two methods of excavation, the so-called Wheeler—Kenyon and Reisner—Fisher methods, can be seen at work and their relative values assessed from the study of the publication (SS I and III). The interested student can pursue this hare for himself, but it is perhaps worth noting that, making allowances for the early date of excavation by the Harvard team there is, *theoretically*, not such a wide gap between the two methods as might be expected. Reisner was able to decern intrusive pits and robber trenches in a homogeneous level; why then were his results not as accurate as Miss Kenyon's? The answer seems to lie in the practical administration of the digging operations. The men in charge of the actual excavation areas were not trained site supervisors but Egyptian foremen, who though they may have been excellent in seeing that the earth was shifted at a reasonable speed, were in no position to put Reisner's theories into practise. Reisner's theories were sound as far as they went, but they were sadly hampered by the unwieldy mechanism of actual digging, inherited in direct line of succession from Petrie, and only somewhat improved upon.

Another important aspect of this dig is, that with the final publication a series of pottery shapes which can be firmly dated to the 9th and 8th centuries B.C. give the student a point where typology and chronology meet. Any such point in the dating of Palestinian finds is extremely important. There are very few sites where such a marriage of historical and archaeological data is possible and it is heartening to know that these chances were not lost [1]). Figs 38 and 39 reproduce the main pottery types of Period I, made during the reign of Omri and Ahab.

HOUSES FROM TELL EL-FARʿAH

Literature:

R. de Vaux, O. P., *La cinquième campagne de fouilles à Tell El-Farʿah, près Naplouse.* Revue Biblique Vol. 62, 1955, pp. 541ff.

A clear impression of the size and plan of Israelite houses can be obtained from the plans of the excavation at Tell el-Farʿah near Nablus under the direction of R. de Vaux O.P. [2]). This site has already produced important evidence from many periods (Chalcol., E.B., M.B. and I.A.) and the excavation is not yet finished. One of the most interesting historical results is that on purely archaeological evidence it has been possible to make the identification of the site with the first capital of Omri, Tirza, acceptable [3]). The site was inhabited before Omri took over power. We know from the O.T. that the king resided there for 6 years (I Kings xvi 23), and during the last years there he started a new building scheme. This was abandoned as soon as Omri decided to build a new capital at the site of the hill of Samaria. It seems that practically the whole of the population of Tirza moved with him to the new site, and the tell of el-Farʿah was abandoned for about three quarters of a century, after which it was built up again on a large scale. This new city was destroyed by the Assyrians in 723 B.C. The material remains at Tell el-Farʿah are in agreement with this.

Niveau III is the pre-Omri level, the town destroyed by this king. This is immediately followed by a period of unfinished building, which in its turn is followed by a slight occupation. Then follows Niveau II representing the town, destroyed by the Assyrians. The

---

[1]) cf. *S.S.* III for the redating of strata from other I.A. sites based on the evidence from Samaria.

[2]) *R.B.* since 1947, Vol. LIVff.

[3]) Cf. *R.B.* Vol 62, (1955) pp. 587-589, and *S.S.* III, pp. 208-ᶜ9.

ceramic evidence suggests that the end of Niveau III coincides with the beginning of the Samaria occupation (Period I) [1].

According to the excavator there are three main levels in the I.A. Niveaux de Tell el-Far'ah:

III	Fin du XIe au début du IXe s.	pre-Omri level.
Batiment inachevé		Omri occupation.
Niv. intermédiaire	IXe s.	slight occupation
II	VIIIe s. - 723 BC	later part of Israelite kingdom.
I	723-600 BC	Assyrian occupation.

The Niveau III houses, reproduced here fig. 40. [2] date from the earlier days of the Northern Kingdom. Inside the excavated area two complete house plans were discovered and part of a third one. The plan is practically the same in the three cases. There is an entrance from the street through a wall leading into the courtyard. The first half of the yard is divided in three parts by two rows of 3 or 4 pillars on stone bases. The central part seems to have had a floor of beaten earth, but in two cases there is a cobbled pavement behind the pillars, and these parts between the pillar bases and the side walls may have been covered by roofs. The second half of the courtyard is flanked by a room on each side, and at the end of the courtyard is a long room with an entrance in the centre or two rooms, each with their own entrance. No traces were found of staircases leading up to a second storey. In the courtyards were found benches, bins and other domestic installations. Two houses, no. 440 and no. 436 are separated by a street, and it seems that there is another street on the east side. The house no. 410A seems to have additions at the east side and the west side. Fig. 41 shows a collection of pottery, found in one room, loc. 418, which can be dated to the end of the period [3].

The 'Bâtiment inachevé', fig. 42, is attributed by the excavator to the rebuilding of the site during Omri's stay there. Père de Vaux notes that no pottery later than level III was found within the walls, which constitute hardly more than the foundations for a new building[4]

---

[1] See n. 3, p. 98.
[2] Cf. *R.B.* 62 (1955), Pl. VI.
[3] Cf. *R.B.* 62, Pl. 16-17.
[4] Cf. *o.c.*, pp. 582-3. Période 2.

Fig. 40. Plan of houses at Tell el-Farʿah, Niveau III

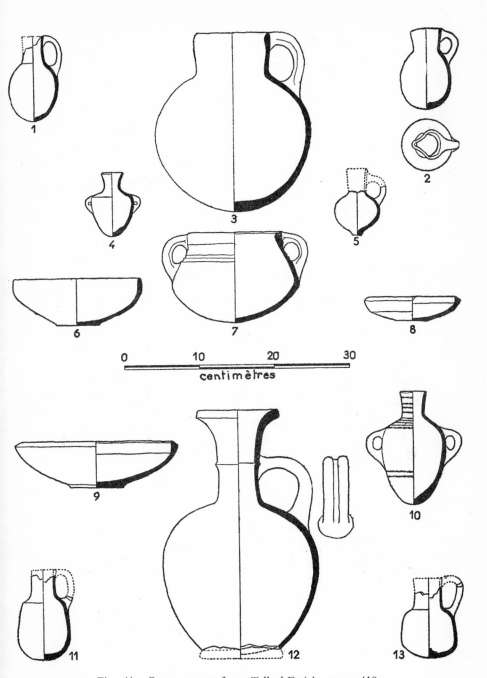

Fig. 41. Pottery types from Tell el-Far'ah, room 418.

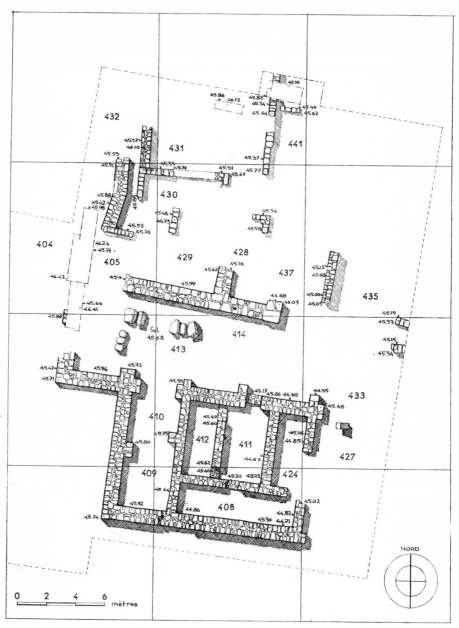

Fig. 42. Plan of the 'unfinished building'; Tell el-Far'ah.

Two houses, fig. 43 [1]), belonging to Niveau II, show that the plan of the houses did not change in the century that elapsed since the end of Niveau III. Only the walls are thicker, consisting of a double course of stones. In no 327 the pillars seem to have been replaced by

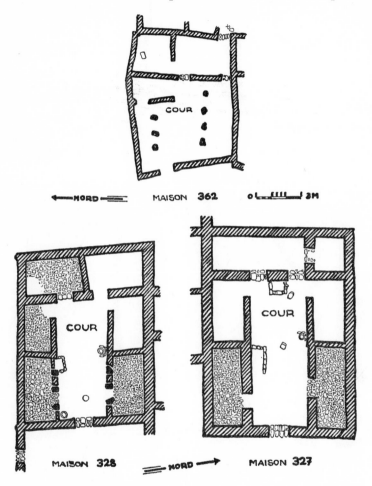

Fig. 43.   Plan of houses at Tell el-Far'ah, Niveau II.

walls, but the pavement situated alongside the courtyard is still typical.

The characteristic pottery from this period is reproduced here figs. 44 and 45. This is comparable with pottery from Samaria Per. IV-VI [2]).

[1]) *R.B.* 59 (1952), Planche XI, detail.
[2]) cf. *S.S.* III, pp. 208f.

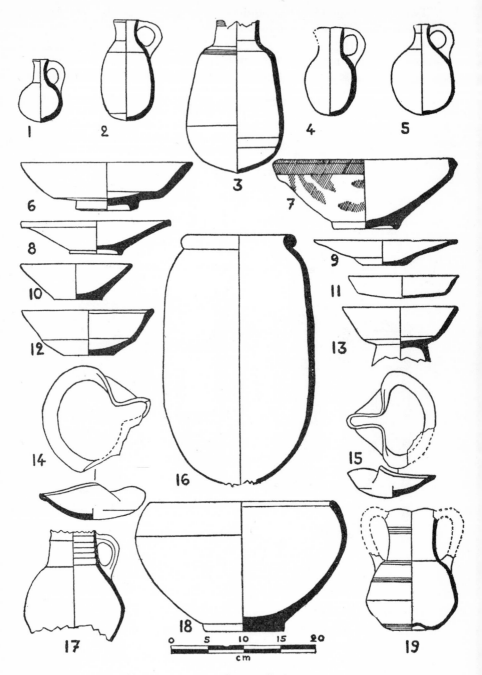

Fig. 44. Pottery types from Tell el-Far'ah. Niveau II.

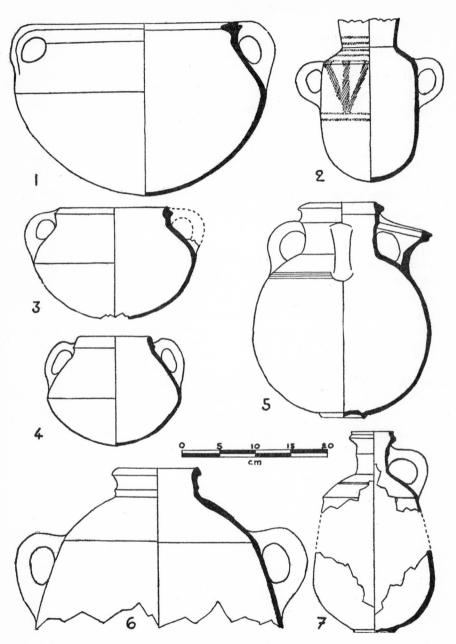

Fig. 45. Pottery types from Tell el-Far'ah. Niveau II.

A Store House at Hazor

Literature:

Hazor I, 1958, II, 1960. The James K. de Rothschild Expedition at Hazor. by
Y. Yadin, Y. Aharoni, R. Amiram, I. Dunayevski, J. Perrot.

When studying an excavation report, the student should always study the paragraphs explaining the system of numbering used by the authors the way loci, findspots etc. are indicated, and in general about the peculiarities of the system of publication, which differ widely with different authors. This is indispensible in the case of the Hazor publication, since the excavation is being published according to the results of each season. This is a rather cumbersome way of publishing, since it necessitates repetitions and corrections of previously published conclusions, so that evidence concerning e.g. the store house is published in Vols. I and II, and will further be discussed in Vols III-IV. Apart from that, the initial numbering system was changed later on, and even in some cases the attribution to a certain stratum is changed in the next volume. (There are also quite a few printing mistakes in Vol. I.) The study of the Hazor publication is recommended because of its valuable results for the Iron Age and the fairly close dating of the finds that can reasonably be trusted to be right, although very little information has yet been published about the stratigraphy proper. For the numbers of loci on the plan, fig. 46, cf. Vol. I, pp. 6-8. Numbers by [I] refer to loci fully discussed in Vol. I. Fig. 46 is taken from the plan Vol. II, Pl. CC, and not Vol. I, Pl. CLXXII.

Tell Waqqâṣ was identified by J. Garstang with biblical Hazor [1]). Garstang made a sounding in the tell, and discovered a row of pillars, which in the present excavation turned out to be part of the store house discussed below. It was proved by Y. Yadin and his collaborators that from the Solomonic period onwards the tell played an important rôle in the history of Israel. The earliest Israelite level is Str. X and our building is attributed to Str. VIII, which dates from the 9th cent. B.C. The building was also in use during Str. VII. It consisted of two parallel wings without direct access to each other. (The meaning of the words 'a corridor or narrow alley runs between them, showing that they are two wings of the same building' [2]) is not clear, since it is no-where supported in the published plans.)

[1]) *o.c.*, Vol. I p. 3. cf. also *A.A.A.*, XIV, pp. 35ff. Garstang excavated at Hazor in 1928.

[2]) *o.c.*, Vol. II, p. 7.

The wings have one wall in common. The orientation is appr. SW.—NE. The larger wing measures 20.75 m by 13.50 m and the width of its walls (foundations) is 1.20 m. These are preserved to a height of 1.30 m and it is suggested that there was a superstructure of mud brick walls. The stone part of the walls rose 0.30-0.60 m. above the floor on the inside. The entrance was found at the W. corner on the N. side; it had a stone paved threshold and the floor near the entrance was also paved with stones. This long hall was lengthwise divided into three parts by two rows of pillars. The row, nearest to the entrance, (the one discovered by Garstang), consisted of 9 pillars, square stones 2 m high, set into the floor to a depth of about 0.50 m. The other row consisted originally of 10 pillars, 4 of which had been removed and re-used after the building was destroyed. The greater part of the floor between these pillars and the nearest wall was paved with slabs of stones in strips, except the east corner of the building, which had an earthen floor like the rest of the building According to the plan, there were two strips of stones along the lines of the pillars, on which shelves had been built between the pillars. This was first taken as an indication that the building could have been a stable. There were very few indications of the purpose of the hall, owing to the sparseness of finds inside it. Some store jars, craters, bowls and small fragments of cups were found. These cups were like the ones found at Beth Shemesh in a store house for grain, and called grain cups, on the presumption that they had been used as measures. Near the NE. side were found some domestic pottery types, including a cooking pot (with an oven), and a stone gaming board, incised on both sides; the excavators suggest that here the watchman or store-keeper used to live.

The other wing was smaller in size, and divided lengthwise into two halls by a wall of equal thickness to the outer walls. The entrance to this wing was close to the entrance of the pillared building. This wing had a completely preserved rough pavement of stones, which in the course of time sank partly in a soft fill underneath, thus revealing the plan of an earlier building.

No indication was found of a second storey. The pillars certainly supported a roof, but why they were used instead of walls, or what the function was of the 'shelves' or 'cellars' between the pillars, remains unexplained. No exact parallels to this building have yet been found, and a full study of the building and its comparisons is to be expected in the last Vol. of the Hazor publication. Since however the excavators exclude the possibility of its being a stable, it is likely to have been a (royal?) store house. Support for this explanation was found in the vicinity of the building, where the Str. X casemates run along the edge of the tell. In Str. VIII they were used for storage. The store house must have been completely empty when it was destroyed, since grain would have been stored in jars, and not on an unpaved floor.

A second floor was laid, attributed to Str. VII, in the Pillared Building, appr. 0.50 m above the first one. At the same time the 'shelves' were rebuilt on a higher level. The second pavement was made of small stones, set far apart.

THE WATER SYSTEM OF EL-GIB

Literature:

> J. B. Pritchard, The Water System of Gibeon; Museum Monographs. The University Museum, Pennsylvania 1961.

During the excavations at tell el-Gib in 1956 and 1957 by J. B. Pritchard the ancient water systems of Gibeon were excavated and studied.

Just as it is nowadays, the supply of a sufficient amount of water was essential for town life in ancient times. All over the Near East excavators have discovered various ways by which towns secured an unhampered access to the nearest water source. The population of a town was threatened with extinction if the access to the water source was blocked by an attacking enemy. Usually the source of water is situated at the lower slopes of the hill on which the town was built. There were two means of securing access to the water during a siege. One way was to protect the path down the slope towards the spring by building a section of the town wall round it. A safer way of securing the supply was to make a tunnel in the rock from inside the city down to the spring. This type of water system is known at other Palestinian sites e.g. at Megiddo, Jerusalem and Gezer. Some of these water tunnels date at least from the Middle Bronze Age, and have been extended and improved upon in subsequent times.

At el-Gib a fairly simple dual system was discovered which is described in short here. The excavator assumes that the earliest attempt to reach the water table is the "pool-and-stairway", found inside the city wall at the N.E. side of the city. This is a roughly circular rock-cut pool, with a diameter of 12.30 m on the N-S axis and 10.30 m on the E-W axis. Along the inside steps lead down to the bottom at 10.80 m below the highest point of the rim. There is a ballustrade along the stairs on the inside, fig. 47.

After the pool was cut to a depth of 10.80 m work was continued in a more economical way by cutting a tunnel with steps down to

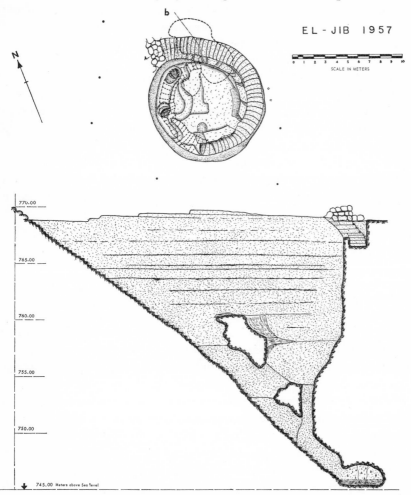

Fig. 47. Plan and section of pool and stairway, Tell el Gib.

the water table. There is a distinct difference in the quality of the finish of this tunnel and the work was obviously more hastily done. Two light shafts from the tunnel to the bottom of the pool provided light to the watercarriers. This tunnel curved round following the plan of the pool above.

The rim of the pool is at 770 m above sea level and the watertable of the hill was reached at $\pm$ 745 m. Here a kidney shaped reservoir was cut in the rock, measuring 6.80 m - 3.40 m with a maximum height of 2.45 m.

The excavator thinks that this project was not very successful and that it was followed by the construction of a tunnel to the source which existed outside and below the city wall.

First a cistern room was constructed (see plan and section fig. 48), the entrance of which could be blocked from the inside to prevent an enemy from entering the city through the water tunnel. Then various sections of the watertunnel were cut, partly by tunneling and partly by trenching from the surface of the slope outside and inside the city wall. Access to the source was thus obtained, which was completely underground and protected against an enemy. At regular intervals niches for lamps were cut in the walls of the tunnel. The tunnel, measured in a horizontal plane, is 45 m long, following a winding course and the drop in elevation is 24.60 m.

Since the dating of the cutting of both water systems depends on the dating of the town walls, further excavation is needed to elucidate this problem. However, from the fill in the pool the excavator concludes a terminus ad quem for its use: late 7th—early 6th century B.C. The building of the city wall preceded the cutting of the stepped tunnel, and the construction of the former is dated 'sometime early in the Iron Age' (o.c. p. 2). Thus it would seem that both water systems belong to the Israelite period.

Thus we find at el-Gib two different attempts to secure a water supply for the city in times of danger. The water works are part of the defence system and the study of the ancient tunnel systems throws light on an important espect of life in antiquity. [1]. As is the case at el-Gib, it is often very difficult to establish the date of the execution of the waterworks and the sequence in which various elements were constructed. Some information concerning the construction seems to be lacking in the publication of these water systems of el-Gib. For example the water channel in the horizontal tunnel has not been planned, nor the stones covering the trenches that form part of the stepped tunnel inside and outside the city wall. To this we return in the following discussion of the sequence of building. Another important piece of information that is missing is the study of the toolmarks

---

[1] cf. A. G. Barrois., *o.c.*, Tome 1. Ch. V. *Installations Hydrauliques.*

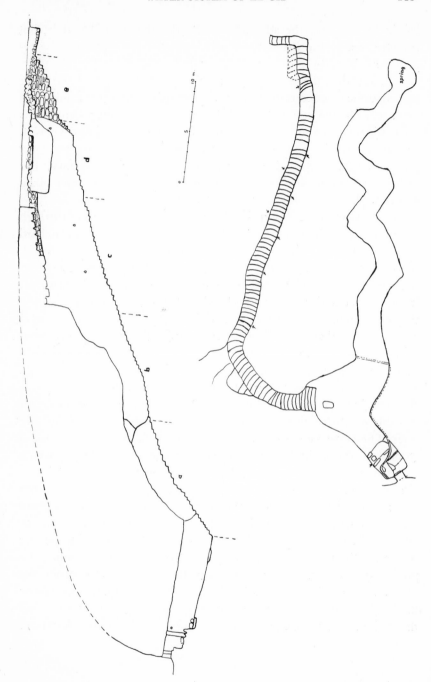

Fig. 48. Plan and section of the water tunnel, Tell el-Gib.

left in the rock by the adzes. Not only the shape of the tools, but sometimes also the metal from which they were made, can be recognized from this sort of research work.

It seems that the excavator's conclusion that the pool-and-stairs preceded the stepped tunnel in time is inconsistent with the published evidence. On the contrary it would seem that the stepped tunnel is the earlier system, and that the pool was planned as an improvement. In the area of the pool and the tunnel to the spring a double town wall was excavated, which cannot yet be dated with certainty. The excavator distinguished between the inner phase and the outer phase of the wall.

The stepped tunnel begins inside the inner phase and is cut through the rock under the outer phase of this wall (cf. section d). Pritchard writes (*o.c.*, p. 7): 'Throughout most of the length of segment d, the engineers were careful to leave 2 m of bedrock as a support between the roof and the base of the heavy city wall above'. However, it seems that under the 'inner phase' they followed another system: they cut a trench from the surface of the rock, measuring approximately 2-3 m so that, if the inner phase existed at that time they would have had to demolish it in the tunnel area before the trench could be cut, and to rebuild it on huge slabs of stones, without the safe margin of two meters of solid rock underneath. It seems obvious that the inner phase did not exist when the tunnel was made. A possible reconstruction of the events could be made on the following lines. The constructors of the inner phase of the wall had to build a stone foundation in one half of the entrance to the tunnel, which was reduced to the width of one meter. Unfortunately no plan of the covering stones of this section has been published. When the inner phase was built the entrance had to be constructed further inside the city. As it was impossible to defend the cistern room effectively against an enemy which was trying to cut off the water supply of the town by blocking the exit of the stepped tunnel, the pool was excavated which was completely inaccessible from the outside. The stairs of the pool lead down to pl.m. 1.5 m below the level of the spring and the distance horizontally is only 5 m from the spring. The pool could well have served its purpose effectively.

CHAPTER SIX

INDUSTRIES AND CRAFTS

In Ch. V we have studied remains of towns and houses in which the Israelites lived. Very little is yet known about the Israelite villages in the mountains and the plains, since excavation has been concentrated on the important places, the towns. It is likely that the farmhouses of the peasants did not differ much from the more simple houses in the towns; the courtyards may have been much larger than the ones in the often overcrowded towns, and there may have been storehouses of a type still unknown to us. There is however no need in the Near East to shelter animals in winter quarters, (in rough weather the animals find shelter in caves) and no possibility for haymaking which would help the animals to survive a succession of very dry years. Hence we must not expect any similarity between the farmer's houses in Palestine and those in colder climates.

In this chapter we deal with the occupations of the Israelites, their 'factories', crafts and industries, as far as archaeology has brought to light any evidence of them. Here we meet a difference with architectural remains: in their building activities ancient man has left permanent traces in the ruins of the buildings. The result of daily activities in the towns, the villages and on the fields has often no permanent character. How did the Iron Age farmer of Palestine plough his land? It would be pure chance if somewhere in Palestine the furrows were found which had been made by an Iron Age plough. This has been the case in some instances in Western Europe, where a field was 'excavated' which still showed the furrows made by the primitive plough of Iron Age man. These traces give the archaeologist useful information about agriculture of the period. In fact these Northern European I.A. furrows resemble those of the present day Arabic peasant's plough in Palestine in the pattern they make across the field. In order to find traces of human activities that usually disappear very soon afterwards, one has to come across a spot where those traces were suddenly 'frozen' by accident, like the furrows mentioned above which were preserved by a mass of wind-blown sand which covered them. Other more permanent products of man's hand are also bound to disappear without leaving any traces behind. Palestine has not a dry climate like Egypt, and objects, made of wood or leather for instance, that are buried in ruins or in tombs, disintegrate in the changing grade of dampness during the seasons. Wooden furniture, that could no longer be used, was likely to have been chopped up and used as firewood in ovens and hearths. There is positive evidence that gold and silver jewelry was remelted by the smiths. Otherwise precious objects were looted when towns were sacked, and they may often have been robbed from tombs already in antiquity, whereas the Iron Age tombs as far as we know were not 'rich' tombs. All this explains why there are not many traces of the art of the goldsmith. Thus from wear and tear, decay or deliberate destruction the vast majority of the products have completely disappeared. Yet the comparatively few objects that did survive and have come to light again give us valuable information concerning the activities of Iron Age man and his technical skill.

Farming was the daily occupation of a good many Israelites. Others, living in towns or in the villages had other employment, and the craftsmen must have formed a large group of the population. In one respect archaeology is bound to give a wrong impression; it has so far traced very few different crafts, whereas there must have been a great variety of technical jobs. But unless their workshops can be recognised from the structures in the soil, or products, archaeology cannot help to trace them. Much general information is preserved about them in the Bible, but we can rarely discover from written sources how the work was done. Most valuable evidence about the work of the scribes can be deduced from the various literary documents in the Old Testament, (style and subject matter) whereas archaeology has not yet been able to provide much additional material information, apart from the ostraca from Lachish and Samaria, some letters and business documents. Music played an important part in Old Testament times, but the soil of Palestine has preserved almost no musical instruments, and we have to turn to contemporaneous pictorial evidence from Egypt or Northern Syria and Mesopotemia to reconstruct them. This is largely due to the material used for certain instruments. If it was entirely made of shell (trumpet) clay (rattle, drum) or metal (tambourine) shapes may survive in the earth whereas wood and skin decay. More is known about the art of weaving, since remains of looms have been found, whereas we know precious little of patterns, apart from what can be seen on non-Palestinian reliefs and tomb paintings.

From this we can deduce what archaeology can hope to find: it depends on the durability of the materials used by the artisans, and partly on the possibilities of chemical analysis. If a storage jar has a dry residue of the old liquid contents in it when it is found, analysis of this residue may tell us more about the substance it contained. The potter is our best known craftsman, since the remains of his fragile product, the sherd, is almost indestructable, much more so than the much less solid product of the blacksmith that corrodes away in the damp soil.

It is only in the perfectly dry climate of the southern deserts and caves that are almost inaccessable that objects are better preserved, but here we have the chance factor that those caves were not used regularly, but only in times of desperation (cf. L.I.N. on the finds of the Bar Kochba revolution). A regularly inhabited cave would moreover only contain the remains of the last occupation period, as in tombs where the best preserved objects are usually those that were buried with the last interment. It is not outside the bounds of possibility that archaeologists could recover the well preserved possessions of a band of marauders who, say, were chased into the desert by a regular Iron Age army, where they hid themselves in a cave from which they could not escape and where they died of thirst. These chance finds can be very valuable, but archaeology cannot concentrate on them and has to make the best of more regular activities. We know then that we cannot expect to find certain products like writings on papyrus etc, because the material used has been almost certainly disintegrated by the agents of the soil such as salts and dampness. Here is a list of raw materials that were used by the craftsman and that had a chance to survive: stone, clay, metal, bone and shell. Other raw materials that have less chance of enduring are: wood, leather, wool and flax, reed, other vegetable material. Most of these materials were used in industries. It is possible that one industry used several raw materials, or that there was coöperation between the craftsmen if they needed each other to make certain products. For instance, the stool maker may have obtained the frames of the stools from the carpenter's shop and finished the product by making the reed or leather seat. The gilded idol was first shaped by the coppersmith from bronze, and then covered in goldleaf by the goldsmith. Stone, whether dressed or undressed, was used by housebuilders, but also by the makers of stone bowls, whereas it was apparently but rarely

used for carving statues etc. A special art was flint making, that died
out during the Iron Age, one of the oldest industries of the world.
Soft limestone was used for making various small objects like spindle
whorls, palettes etc. Another type of stone, closely related to
Egyptian alabaster, was worked in Palestine for finer vessels. Here
we have already a number of different specialities, in which stone
was the basic raw material. Clay was mainly used by the potter.
It was also used by builders of houses etc. The furnace of the
metal workers was made of clay, and some of his tools like
blowpipe and crucible, which he may have made himself since they
did not need to be fired in an oven before they could be used. Clay
was also used for his moulds. The housewife used clay to make her
little bread oven and benches in courtyards were often made of
clay, as were cupboards and pigeon holes. Like most of the types
of stone needed in daily life, clay was a material that was amply
available in most parts of Palestine. This was not the case with metal,
iron, copper, silver and gold. Whereas silver and gold do not seem
to have played an important role in the daily life of the Israelite and
only became important for the royal courts and their economy (or
in cases of tribute to foreign powers), the other metals, iron and
bronze were wanted by craftsmen and farmers for tools, and by the
army for weapons. In order to obtain large quantities of raw
materials, the kings had to maintain their power over trade routes
and sources or else the price would go up considerably and supply
might even come to a full stop. Iron working was a completely new
industry at the beginning of the Iron Age and, as is stated by the
Old Testament, it was the monopoly of the Philistines until the
reign of king David. Trade in iron and bronze were a matter of
international politics and also of wars with neighbouring countries.

There was always a sufficient supply of bone for bone tools. A number
of them may have been home made and were used for domestic
purposes, such as needles, pins, spindles and whorls. A bone tool,
used by potters can easily be shaped from a rib, but other objects may
have been made by a special craftsman, for example, the bone pendants
of a shape that is only found in Iron Age Palestine, which are thought
to have been amulets. With the flint industry the working of bone
tools belongs to the oldest industries of mankind, and bone tools
were not replaced completely before the age of synthetic products
of modern industry. Bone was a medium for artistic work also.
Bone has much more chance of surviving in the Palestinian soil

than other organic materials, especially if it had been to a certain degree calcinated in a fire that destroyed a building or a whole town.

Shell was also used, and as far as it came from the Red Sea, was a trade product. Shells, used by potters, may well have been taken from fossil beds in the rocks. Shells were used as ornaments but also for other purposes, according to size and shape.

The less durable materials were organic matter. First there was wood of various kinds, expensive wood imported from the Lebanon (cedar,) to kindling from bushes, only fit for the fire. It had very many applications, in building and construction, for tools, furniture, musical instruments, saddles etc. Leather was equally used for many purposes, watersacks, shoes, saddles, ropes, slings, in parts of the soldier's armour, caps, reins etc. Wool was used for clothes, saddles, tents etc. and reed, found near the watercourses, was used for the construction of roofs, for baskets and mats, flutes and furniture.

During the more prosperous times of the Kingdoms, more expensive raw materials could be imported for luxury articles, like the murex (for purple dye) and precious stones. (Cf. the list of articles imported by king Solomon from overseas, 1 Kings x 22). On the whole, however the population depended on what the country itself had and produced for all its needs. This does not mean, however, that there was not a wide variety of possibilities. People living on the land know what they can do with herbs and plants. A date palm was not only good for its dates, but the leaves were used as well as the stones and the hard leaves that protect the young shoots. Animals were hunted or trapped for a special purpose, if only for the hair of a certain part of the body for a special type of brush, to make a special dye or a charm. The cosmetic 'industry' used many different raw materials. Assuming that medicine in Israel was not entirely a question of magic, it is bound to have been a science of roots, leaves, animal anatomy, excrements of certain animals etc. Evidence of advanced surgery in the Iron Age comes from Lachish where three trepanned skulls were recovered. This would have been executed with a hammer and copper chisel, the normal instruments used for this operation up to the 18th century A.D. For one thing is certain, however limited the possibilities of the raw materials may seem to us, living in a synthetic age, the 'primitive' craftsman and woman knew the existing materials of their trades extremely well, and did infinitely more with them than we can imagine. Hence we should not a priori think of an Iron Age town or village as a simple community however primitive it might seem to be to a modern observer. Nor can we judge the degree of 'development' from certain examples of folk art. Products that do not appeal to us may be the result of highly developed technical skill, working with a simple raw material. We will only be able to understand the height of a culture in its material aspect when we know *how the problems of daily life were solved.* To a certain extent this can be studied from the material remains, and if we can understand why a building that has a curious architectural feature was made that way or why the farmer did not improve his 'primitive' plough. In most cases there is an answer to such questions and we will find that the Iron Age culture in its full development was a reasonable answer to the problems which generations had struggled to solve; We should not forget that those problems were primarily problems of survival: safety, unity of the tribes, drought and famine, diseases of humans, animals and crops, the lack of natural rich sources. Moreover, the Old Testament tells us of this struggle in the light of the demands of a unique religious conception which archaeology cannot ignore, nor fully evaluate. The second Commandment must have had a strong influence on shapes and decorations and prohibited the use of certain objects, whereas it may have stimilated other cultural aspects that are the least likely to be found in excavation, like music, poetry and the interpretation of history in story telling.

Naturally there were other employments besides the working of raw materials. There were tradesmen, either living permanently in a shop, or travelling from place to place. There were many officials, appointed by the court or by local governors, the standing armies and all the people attached in various ways to the cult in Jerusalem or to local sanctuaries. Their work hardly leaves any special traces in the soil that can be recognised. It is very difficult in many cases to decide what was the purpose of a workshop once it is uncovered. There were sometimes round stone pavements in houses of the early Iron Age at Deir 'Allā which were clearly not floors, but laid for some other purpose. There were no indications however from the pottery or other objects to show what purpose they served. The potter's workshop can more readily be recognised from the way it is arranged than the workshop of a carpenter who did not use any stone or clay-built installations, and whose tools, made of wood and metal, may have decayed. Moreover, finished products of an industry are normally found distributed in the houses of the users, and only a violent destruction or abandonment of a workshop preserves the indications needed for an accurate interpretation by the archaeologist.

The study of ancient techniques will help us in certain cases to explain the use of a room more closely. Chemical analysis may also help in cases where traces of vegetable matter or remains of unorganic materials that were left over during the work are found. We must reckon with the possibility that many workshops were situated outside the city walls and liable to have been eroded away completely or simply not found by the excavator. The fact that workshops and ordinary living rooms cannot be distinguished from each other in many cases is also partly explained by the fact that the tools of the trade were often very primitive. A crooked nail becomes an experts tool in the hands of a present day chauffeur in the Near East, and the finest works of art of the goldsmith have been worked with the most unexpected tools.

There is one more general aspect to be taken into account. The craftsman in the Near East stands in the tradition of his trade which is usually a very old one, handed down from generation to generation. Often he has a deep knowledge of his material and he knows exactly what he can do with it and what he cannot. There may even be a jealously guarded formula which only his family knows. But apart from that, he is a very industrious man who works under the most primitive conditions, often in poor light and with hardly any room to move, but accepting his life and small profit. His is a very different character from the farmer or shepherd, since he is constantly producing a product which has the quality of hand-made wares and often a sort of beauty which though perhaps not intentionally created, is assessed by him by refusing to produce wares inferior to his family's traditional standard. His work is apt to remain conservative. On the whole much more work could be done from what is already known and by careful excavation to produce more information about daily occupations of the Israelites. Since the best known craft is the potter's, this will be dealt with in some detail. It is clear that here also more study could be done, especially in view of the techniques employed by the potter. Some other industries will also be discussed, in as far as present archaeological evidence allows.

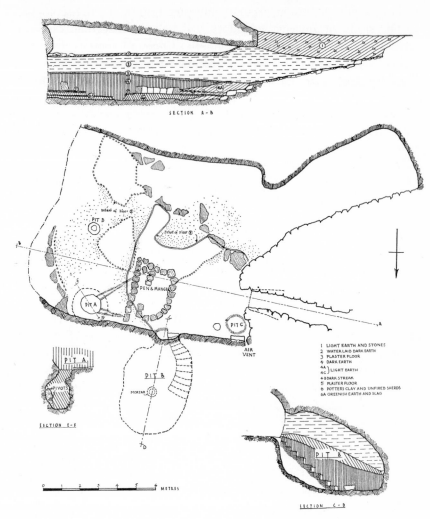

Fig. 49.   Potter's workshop in Cave 4034, Lachish.

A POTTER'S WORKSHOP FROM LACHISH

Literature:

Lachish IV, pp. 291-193.

Fig. 49 shows the plan of the cave in which the potter worked [1]).
(Pl. IX-X) A sloping passage leads to a large cave. This cave could
only be partly excavated owing to the bad state of the roof at the

---

[1]) *Lachish* IV, Plates, Pl. 8 and 49. Pl. 92. Situation of the cave cf. *o.c.*, Pl. 128.

east side. The cave was cut in soft lime stone under a hard layer which formed the roof. A long extension of the cave to the west was blocked by stones on the outer side.

The section through the fill of the cave shows 6 layers of deposit. According to Miss Tufnell a neolithic or chalcolithic arrowhead, found in the mud fill of pit B might indicate an early occupation. Since however this mud fill dates from after the period in which the cave was used as a potter's work shop, which is at least until the fall of the L.B.A. city, it seems more likely that this object was washed inside with the mud.

Layer 1 contained some Roman sherds, which got in before the entrance was completely sealed, and does not represent an occupation level. Layer 2 is also not an occupation deposit. Caves with an inward sloping entrance are bound to become filled with clay or sand washed in by regular flooding, unless the cave is in use and the entrance protected by a high step.

Layer 3 (on the section A-B) is a fragment of a plaster floor without any dating material.

Layer 4, dark earth, which contained many sherds. Just above floor 5 there were several pieces of a bowl painted with palms and zigzags [1]) and other vessels represented in the fill were storage jars with red painted bands, and pilgrim flasks with burnished cream slip and painted spirals. Seven pieces of Iron Age hand burnish on red slip are typical of an early stage in that technique.

Layer 5 is marked in section A-B as a plaster floor. The description mentions only the stones (shaded in section and plan) stating that they were evidence of use of the cave as a sheep-fold. Some sherds of layer 4 (presumably the E.I.A. ones) should belong to this phase of occupation. The pen and manger were connected with pit A by two drainage channels, according to the excavators since floor 5 was broken away around this pit and part of fill 4 was found in the top of this pit. However, most of this pit was filled with earlier debris. On the other hand it seems that pit B (an extension of the cave) was used as refuse pit (see section C-D), and the drainage channel may have been an earlier feature.

Layer 6 was a thick deposit of compact clay over the floor of the cave, containing quantities of unbaked sherds which were much less common near the entrance. The excavators observed that the possible

---

[1]) Cf. *Lachish* II, pottery types no. 117 and 125.

position of the potter's kilns may be indicated by a widening streak of greenish earth and slag, layer 6 a, which was most clearly defined in the furthest recesses of the cave, the unexcavated area. It is certainly not impossible that kilns were built in the cave. The inner mantle of the kiln would have been built of mud-bricks and had to be renewed at regular intervals, and the funnels would have been cut through the roof of the cave. The slag is the molten clay from the mantle of the kiln, which had to be broken out of the kiln. Kilns of this type have the great advantage that the surrounding rock protects the kiln from loosing heat. At the same time however, the heat may in the long run have caused the collapse of the roof in that part of the cave.

Pit C was about 1 m deep. There was a stone slab, explained as the seat of the potter, when he was turning pots on a wheel in the pit. There was a light entrance on the right hand side above the pit. Here remains of a potter's wheel were found, two tenons, one basalt and one limestone. Complete sets of this type of potter's wheel have been found e.g. by Sellin at Shechem and recently at Hazor. When the two parts fit well and some olive oil is used as a lubricant, the wheel will turn quite well. However it seems improbable that such a wheel was fitted in the pits (pit D) as the excavators suggest [1]), unless a wooden construction was fitted to the upper stone disk to enable the potter to turn the wheel with his feet. If the wheel was hand operated, it must have been placed on a shelf over the pit, to give the potter a better position. It is assumed by the excavators that the wheel was foot operated [2]).

Pits C and D may have been places where the pots were thrown on the wheel. Pit A could have been a water reservoir. The clay could be prepared, cleaned, slipt and mixed outside the cave in the open air, but the prepared clay had to be stored inside to prevent drying out too quickly, and this may also have been the function of pit A or of pit B, which provided the potter with a large storage space. In order to ensure an equal temperature in the workshop, the potter apparently had to rebuild and partly block the entrance, which explains the stone construction at the west side.

The pottery contents of the store room, pit B, consisted of shapes known from the Fosse temple III, the latest occupation of L.B.A.

---

[1]) Cf. A. Rieth, 5000 *Jahre Töpferscheibe*, Konstanz, 1960. p. 33.
[2]) *o.c.*, p. 91.

Lachish. Since it was the porter's stock, it marks the end of this pottery. Some important finds were the fragment of an unbaked figurine, showing that this potter made those objects, probably for the sanctuary, and there were also imitations of imported L.B. wares.

Potters tools. A type of pot, found in the cave is called the 'potters jar' (Plate X), apparently made by the potter for his own use in the work shop. Amongst the finds from pit A was a sherd with red ochre. This was used for the decoration of pottery, and usually applied to the pot before firing it [1]). Apart from the stone tenons there were a stone mortar, pottery templates [2]), used to smooth the surface of the pot while it was turned on the wheel, a bone point for cutting off surplus clay from the rim and pebbles probably used for burnishing the leather-hard pots before firing them. The mortar was used for grinding either colouring material, or crushing material like shells, flint or limestone to be mixed with the clay. Templates are found on I.A. sites. They are always worn on one or two sides by being used to smooth the surface of the wet pot on the wheel. The Lachish examples were made of potsherds, shaped to fit the purpose. At Deir 'Allā one specially made by the potter for this purpose was found. Shells and pebbles were used to smooth or burnish the surface of vessels after they had been put aside to dry and had become leather hard. Pots treated in this way will show a shiny surface after being fired in the kiln.

Although this potter's workshop belongs to the end of the L.B.A. we can assume that many Israelite potters worked under the same conditions as there are even to-day in many parts of the Near East potters running a thriving business under very similar conditions. The potter needs a good deal of space for preparing his clay, storing fresh supplies, and fuel for the kiln, drying the various types of pots before they could be fired, storing pots that needed a second treatment after the clay had become leather-hard etc., apart from the space needed for the kilns. The room in which the pots were turned on the wheel can have been very small. An even temperature in which to dry pots, and underground kilns were very important. Normally there would not have been sufficient room for the pottery within the town wall and added to this was the danger of a general conflagration in the city should the of firing kiter get out of control. Apart from that, the potter needs a good deal of water.

---

[1]) *o.c.*, p. 140.

[2]) These objects are colled felukas in the Megiddo publications.

In a potter's shop many members of the family could find employment. Clay and water had to be collected as well as fuel for the kiln. The clay had to be mixed and left until a certain degree of dampness was reached, and then it had to be taken up and made into lumps of a certain size, according to what type of pot was going to be made next. The potter threw enough pots to fill a kiln, and these pots had to be put away to dry further, and some of them had to have a second treatment on the wheel, after which they had to dry again. As soon as enough pots were made to fill a chamber in the kiln, the pots were piled up in the kiln and the kiln was fired, which needed an expert man to guarantee not only the right degree of heat, but also a well-regulated temperature right through the process of firing. All these jobs could be done by different people, and the actual throwing of pots could also be done by more than one man, each of whom specialized in certain types.

POTTERY STUDY

Pottery making is a craft in which tradition plays an important rôle. To begin with, the potter must know which locally obtainable clay is the best to be used for his purpose, and this already is a matter of long experience. The Iron Age potters may not have done much to season the clay or to slip it, but they knew what to mix with clays to make a heat resistant cooking pot. Iron Age wares are usually well fired, and this points to well-made kilns and intelligent firing.

Since so much initial study of Palestinian archaeology has to be devoted to pottery forms and very little is published about the potters techniques in the Iron Age, something has to be said here about the art of throwing and shaping a pot. This will help students in their study of various types of pottery and the comparison with published material in the excavation reports. It should not be forgotten that the study of pottery can only be properly done from pottery collections [1].

The Iron Age potter made pots which are quite distinctly different from those of the previous period. The difference in shape between pottery from the two periods can be studied from many publications [2], but the technique cannot always be seen in the drawings

---

[1] cf. Appendix,
[2] cf. W. F. Albright, *Tell Beit Mirsim*, A.A.S.O.R. Vols XIII and XXI-XXII.

of pots. The most characteristic part of a pot, found in great quantities on excavated sites, are the rims, usually with part of neck and body of the pot still attached. These rims can be classified. One can sort the main bowl rims, krater-rims, store-jar rims, cooking pot rims and each of these types can be subdivided. After a training in the field the archaeologist can sort 90% of the rims found in a season into main types and a good deal of subdivisions without much trouble. The remainders are usually odd and rare shapes. Usually the excavation reports do not give more information about the pottery than shapes, a description of the ware and decoration, and findspot, but no study of the techniques. The shape is indeed best described by a drawing, and the purpose is to provide the student of reports with comparative material. More could be done however, to describe a pot technically.

A rim can be a plain straight rim or be profiled. A straight rim whether upright or flaring can be shaped by hand, and some profiles, but not all can also be formed with the fingers of both hands on the pot as it turns. While studying the cooking pots from Deir 'Alla it was found that the height of the rims of all types and from all the different I.A. levels had more or less a standard size. Very few types had a rim of the height of the width of 4 fingers, and those rims were thin and straight. By far the most rims were half this size, the width of two fingers, and they were profiled rims. A third variation was that the top half of this type was cut off with a pin leaving a practically flat top.

The profiled rims could be roughly divided into upright rims and inturned rims, turning in the same direction as the upper part of the wall of the pot. Both types could have the same profiles. The simplest profile was one made by pressing two fingers against the outside of the rim, and one finger of the left hand inside as a support against the rim. The result was a 'double' rim, or a rim and a sharp profile underneath, formed by the impression of the two fingers against the outside. If the shoulder of the pot was well shaped, the profile would also be clear. The process of shaping the rim would push it slightly upwards, and the link between shoulder and rim would take an *s* shape, which tends to be much thinner than the wall of the pot. A more complicated profile, e.g. a band under the first rim, can not have been made by hand and was achieved by pressing a rib, made of bone or wood, against the outside of the rim, or simply a bone pin, This gives a wide variety of rim shapes, but from an analysis of the techniques applied a system of initial sorting of the rims can be achieved. When the study of the cooking pot rims was finished at Deir 'Allā it was found that in many cases the same techniques were employed with other types. Thus the rims of large storage jars, that are quite different in appearance from those of the cooking pots, came quite close to them in point of view of technique, and in certain cases could be matched with cooking pot rims, apart from ware and diameter. They all measure the width of 4 fingers in height, but whereas the cooking pot rims have sometimes been cut to half that width or folded over to gain the same effect, the jar rims kept that height. But here again a well shaped shoulder and a clearly defined angle between shoulder and rim resulted in a clear profile of the rim, whereas a vague profile was the result of the shoulder turned up at the rim without an appreciable angle. These rims could be divided according to the same principles as the cooking pot rims: the ones that were made by hand only or worked with tools.

Some of the techniques are well known. The pilgrims flask is made of two bowls fitted together along the rim, and a neck inserted on the top where the rims link, by cutting out a hole in which it was fitted. Other techniques have as yet hardly been studied at all. There is the question whether the cooking pot can be made in one go, for owing to the quality of the clay used for it, this seems virtually impossible. Some of the cooking pots from Deir 'Alla show signs that they have been built up by hand first and then turned on a wheel to smooth them after they had been allowed to dry leather-hard. The study of some bases of cooking pots showed that another technique was also used: the rim had been made first with the upper part of the body and, with the rest of the unshaped clay attached to it, was then allowed to dry leather hard. The remaining lump of clay would then still have been wet enough to be turned. The pot was put upside down on the wheel, on a cone of clay made to fit the rim, and then the lower part of the pot was made, first as a cylinder which was closed while being shaped to the proper form. This closing of the bottom after the rim has been made leaves a characteristic impression in the centre of the base, which had to be smoothed away afterwards, since the inside of a cooking pot had to be smooth all round. It turned out too that many bases of storage jars clearly showed signs of having been turned in two parts, probably from one lump of clay in the above described manner. At present, this can only be studied from actual potsherds, since these aspects are neither described nor expressed in drawings in the publications. Yet it would seem that the study of the technique applied to a pot could make the classification of pottery shapes more certain. This type of classification should however never be taken as an indication of the development of shapes, unless another factor has been added to it: the study of the stratification in which the pots were found [1]).

In excavation reports there is always a large section devoted to the study of the pottery found on the site. The chronology of the site is based on this study of the pottery finds, and comparisons with pottery found and dated on other sites. The pottery study contains illustrations with conventionalized drawings of the various pottery types. These drawings are either made from complete pots or from fragments. If enough fragments are found to make up a section of the pot from the base to the top, then the whole pot can be reconstructed in drawing. From the existing remains of a rim the diameter can be measured with the help of a simple device. The pot is drawn with a vertical line through the axis, and one half of the pot shows the outside, the other half a vertical cut through the wall of the pot, showing the inside and the thickness of the wall. In this way decoration on the outside as well as on the inside of bowls can be shown, including burnishing. The description of the pot is usually confined to remarks about ware (hard, medium or soft), the colour of the clay at the surface and sometimes in the core, the mixture of the clay as far as can be seen with the eye, and special remarks (use of slip, etc.). One sometimes finds in an appendix a spectrographic analysis of the clay of some pots.

The pottery catalogue can be arranged in different ways. Sometimes one finds all the pots of one category but of all periods dealt with in one paragraph. Other publications give the pottery from each stratum or level and sometimes groups of pottery found in one locus, like in graves, are assembled together. The disadvantage of this last method seems to be that certain types have to be published several times, that is to say for each level in which they occur. Yet this is far better than the first more 'economical' method, where it seems that often one pot is taken as an example, which cannot really be matched with pots from other strata, although they may resemble it. No two pots are exactly the same, and some system has to be found

---

[1]) For the potter's technique see B. Leach, *A Potter's Book*, London, 1951; Kelso and Palin Thorley *A.A.S.O.R.*, Vol. XXI-XXII.

to simplify the typology, but it is very important that groups of pottery from one level can be studied as a unity. Moreover two seemingly identical pots can have been made in completely different techniques, and if taken as one type, give misleading evidence.

While studying the pottery of Palestine the student should keep in mind that the nature of the raw material, the clay, limits the possibilities of the potter. Some Palestinian clays are good plastic clays, but usually a special treatment is needed before a good quality potter's clay is obtained. The clay then has to be left lying in the open for a long time, to allow the elements to break up the lumps of clay, and afterwards the clay has to be slipped in a number of successive basins to obtain a fine clay. Usually however the Palestinian potter did not do much to improve the clay in this way. Mixing clay with river sand, ground shell, flint or limestone was however a common practise. A high lime content of a clay lowers the maximum temperature at which it can be fired before it disintegrates, and consequently pots made of that type of clay are softer than others. Clay for cooking pots was probably mixed with ashes in order to facilitate the throwing on the wheel. It had to be mixed with a fair amount of grit to make it heat resistant. The typical cooking pot ware can be immediately recognised and distinguished from other wares.

Though limited by the nature of the clay he used, the I.A. potter usually was a very skilled thrower, who could turn small pots from a cone of clay, or make enormous storage jars. He knew several ways of making a round base and on the whole he made a better base than his late Canaanite predecessor, and he made a much wider variety of rim shapes.

All Palestinian clays contain a certain amount of iron. This produces the red colour of the fired wares when a sufficient amount of air is let into the kiln during the firing. 'Reduced' firing would change the colour of the pots. Amongst other possiblities of influencing the result of the firing was treatment of the pot with a fine slip, a technique often found in the early Iron Age. The making of a slip requires much experience since the slip and the clay must shrink equally during the firing, or else the slip will not adhere to the pot. This slip could be burnished with a smooth, hard object (bone, shell), and would have a shiny surface after firing. After 900 B.C. burnishing was often done on a wheel. Painted decoration is not often found on Iron Age pots. If the pot was painted before firing then inorganic material (ocre) was used. On the whole, however, decoration is scarce, though the pots are of a very good shape. The ordinary wheel burnished water decanter of the Iron Age II is a perfect example of the potter's skill and ability, which stands comparison with any of the better pottery of other cultures.

OTHER USE OF CLAY

Clay was not only used by the potters, but also by builders and others in areas such as the Jordan valley where there is an abundance of clay more readily accessible than stone. Houses, courtyard walls, sheds etc. could be built almost exclusively from clay. Fig. 9 shows the remains of houses of which only the roof was constructed with another material: wood, and there may have been wooden doors. No stone was used for these houses. The bricks of these early Iron Age houses are approximately $60 \times 40 \times 10$ cms and laid without any kind of mortar between them. Some walls were made of well mixed clay bricks and these proved to be stronger than bricks that were made of very badly mixed clay. That even bricks were sometimes reused could be seen in walls that had many differently coloured bricks, which were certainly not made at the same time and place.

Iron Age roofs were constructed with a thick layer of clay, as has been pointed out already, and are generally supposed to have been flat. It is perfectly possible to construct a domed roof with bricks and without any wood, but the walls would have been twice as thick as they usually are, had they supported domed roofs.

Often one finds traces of a plaster finishing to the mud brick walls. Clay with a plaster finish was also used for benches, platforms, cupboards etc., thus replacing wooden constructions. Clay ovens were probably made by the housewifes themselves. They presented a curious problem to the excavators at Deir 'Allā. They have a diameter of $\pm$ 50 cms and are built up in coils of wet clay like a straw beehive. Although no undamaged oven was found, it was clear that there was only a narrow opening. The inside was more or less 'ringburnished' as a result of regular clearing out of the ashes with a potsherd. The oven baked itself while being used. Often there were several ovens in succession, which became necessary not only from wear but from the rather rapid rise of the courtyard level. It turned out however that from constantly scraping the inside to clear it from ashes, the bottom of the oven became deeper, and in cases where a fine distinction between levels of the courtyard was needed in connection with a general change in plan of the house it was extremely difficult to attribute the oven to the correct courtyard level. After heating the oven and than extinguishing the fire by covering the opening, the bread could be rapidly baked.

The blacksmith used clay to make crucibles. These were hand made and baked hard from the inside from the heat of the molten metal poured into them. Their life must have been fairly short for they eventually burnt right through and had to be replaced. Sometimes the potter made clay toys for children. Miniature pots are usually considered as toys. Clay rattles may not have been toys but used in processions. It is curious to note that no clearly recognisable pottery drums have been reported. Many objects connected with the cult must have been made of clay. So were loom weights.

STONE AND ITS USE

Stone, used and often shaped and worked by human hand, is found at all Iron Age sites. Most common are river boulders, used as they were found in the wadis for foundations of town walls, public buildings and houses. Stones of various kinds of rock are carried down by seasonal turrents and deposited in the wadi beds. A number of these stones come from geological beds that are eroded by the rainwater. These stones were also used for building walls without being dressed. Building strong walls in this way is an art in itself, which needs experience. The shape of each stone has to be taken into account when being laid, and small stones or stone chips are wedgled between them as support [1]. A well built stone wall could last for a very long time, certainly longer than a brick wall. The wall could be plastered after a smooth surface had been made of mud. Expert stone builders can still be found in Arabic villages to-day as well as builders of mud brick houses. Undressed stones were also used for stone benches, in workshops for various installations and pavements both inside and outside houses.

Stone masons knew how to dress stone and in certain periods and for specific purposes stone was quarried and properly shaped, as it was done under Phoenician influence at Samaria by the Omrides. The excavation reports use the present day Arabic names for certain

---

[1] Cf. *The fortress of Gibea*, *A.A.S.O.R.*, XXXIV, 1960, PL 34.

types of stone found and quarried in Palestine: nari is a hard crust of lime, the result of the weathering of a limestone bed, and often roofs of caves consist of nari. Mizzi and howr are also limestone rocks and from these the dressed stones are usually cut [1]). Most of the surface rock in Palestine consists of various types of limestone, which is comparatively soft stone. In historical times stone was quarried with metal tools, and it is sometimes possible to deduce from the tool's marks which shape the chisel had that was used and a careful examination of the surface sometimes leads to the discovery of fragments of metal of which the tool was made, especially bronze. The same imprint from the tool is usually to be found in the walls of rock cut cisterns and tombs.

STONE MASON'S WORK AT SAMARIA

Literature:

Samaria-Sebaste I, *The Buildings* Ch. II, 1, A-C.

It is assumed by the excavators that the higher courses of the walls found round the summit of the hill of Samaria were made of sun dried bricks. These have disappeared, but the socles of masonry on which these walls were reared were found in many places and considered as masterpieces of the builder's craft. The foundations were laid in rock-cut trenches. This fact enabled the excavators to trace the course of these walls even where the stones had been taken away in antiquity (robber trenches). The lay-out shows a geometrical regularity of planning. The stones are very closely fitted and bonded in a more or less regular pattern: at the bottom of the walls they are generally laid on edge as headers: in the upper courses stretchers, also laid on edge alternate sometimes with single headers, frequently with pairs of headers, occasionally with three or more (*o.c.*, p. 5).

A remarkable feature is that the courses are perfectly horizontal and the vertical joints perpendicular [2]). The stones were split off in the quarry, in a roughly rectangular shape and then brought to the site where further shaping was done.

The face of the stones was dressed smooth. The bottom courses however showed clearly how the masons went to work. Here bosses were left in the middle with a marginal draft which does not run round the boss but along the top of it and on one or two sides. These

---

[1]) Cf. *Lachish* III, Text, pp. 36-38 plus the literature there.

[2]) cf. Fisher in *Harvard Expedition*, p. 105f.

margins turned out to have been the remains of edges that were smoothed to receive the guiding lines which the masons drew to show how much had to be cut off. Several of these lines have survived. They were made apparently by snapping a taut cord smeared with red paint. For drawing a vertical line a plummet was used and for horizontal lines a plummet and a square. The stones often show clearly the marks of the adzes used by the masons. These adzes were apparently made of iron.

The care which was taken by the masons is clearly illustrated in the treatment of the foundation trenches. These trenches varied with the nature of the rock. Where the rock was hard enough, only a shallow cutting was made, but where it was decayed, the trench was enlarged until solid rock was encountered, and the cavity was carefully

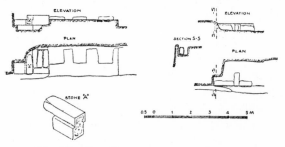

Fig. 50.   Israelite stone-cutting, Samaria.

filled with dressed stones. The stones varied in size except that the height of the stones of each course was exactly the same for each stone. Figs 50 and 51 show the method of construction of this type of wall [1]).

It seems that this careful method of building was neither widespread nor long lived. Soon at Samaria the walls receive a much coarser treatment, and this may well indicate that after the initial help of the Phoenician craftsmen the local masons retired to their own standards of work. It is moreover clear that only court and state buildings were executed in this fine standard of craftsmanship. Comparisons with buildings from Palestine and Syria are given in S.S.I, and since this publication more examples have come to light. For the average Israelite this type of work was far too costly to be realized. (Pl. VII, b).

---

[1]) *S.S.* I, Figs 3 and 4.

OTHER USE OF STONE

Cisterns. As soon as a water-proof plaster was discovered, cisterns could be made. This seems to have happened early in the Iron Age. Digging in the soft limestone rock is possible even with bronze tools, but this type of rock is porous. Once it became possible to make the walls of rock-cut pits waterproof, water and other liquids could be stored this way. This was especially important in two cases: certain industries needed a good water supply and towns that did not have a well inside the walls or a protected access to a water source at the foot of the hill on which they were built, now could store a large amount of rain water in case of invasion. An enormous and

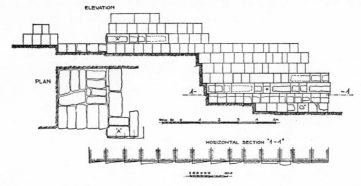

Fig. 51. Israelite wall on south side, Samaria.

still unfinished water reservoir has been found in Iron Age Lachish, and another large Iron Age cistern has been found in el-Gib. Smaller Iron Age cisterns and reservoirs have been found on various sites, as at Samaria and Tell Beit Mirsim [1]). Here pits were dug through the deposits of earlier occupation until bed rock was reached, and there the reservoir was cut into the rock. Stone masonry was used to protect the opening of the reservoir.

Caves. Natural caves were inhabited right through the history of man in Palestine, from the earliest times onward. Caves were adjusted to special purposes, like the potter's cave at Lachish, and were used as sheep folds but also as dwellings. During the Iron Age caves were also used as tombs. At least since Chalcolithic times artificial caves or rock cut chambers were made to serve as tombs. These tombs were often used again and again by taking out the earlier

---

[1]) cf. *Tell Beit Mirsim, Iron Age.* A.A.S.O.R. XXI-XXII, § 39.

contents. Presumably a new type of rock cut tomb was added to the existing types in the Iron Age [1]).

Vessels and other implements. After the invention of pottery making, stone vessels remained in use for certain purposes. No clay vessel could be made hard enough to replace the stone mortars, and in Iron Age kitchens stone vessels are found beside the pottery vessels. Also the industries used stone bowls, mortars etc. In the kitchen dried roots, nuts and other vegetable ingredients were crushed in mortars to be mixed with the food. The potter crushed baked potsherds, lumps of ochre etc. for his work. Bowls were often made in a 'cheap' way; a stone (often lime stone) was chosen which needed the least work to be done to shape it into a bowl. There are also carefully made stone bowls, shaped into round or square dishes, sometimes on three short legs. Often basalt was used for this purpose or other volcanic stones. Mortars and pestles were usually made of volcanic rock. The old craft of making stone bowls was certainly not lost in the Iron Age. A special use of stone was for the querns (mill stones) of this period, found in many houses. Pl. XI.

Small objects. Local and imported stones were used for many purposes. Flint was used for three kinds of objects. Often flint balls, roughly shaped and slightly bigger than a tennis ball, are found on Iron Age sites. They may well have been used in war as ammunition. Another object, the blade of which was made of flint is the sickle, which dies out during the Iron Age. This is the last survival of the old flint industries, so characteristic of the whole Stone Age. This sickle was gradually replaced by metal ones. It consisted of a number of blades with one indented edge, set in a crescent shaped wooden handle and cemented in it. The edges often show a high 'polish' which is in fact the result of a long use of cutting standing corn. These flint implements have often been found Another flint tool, that certainly existed was the knife used in rituals (circumcision). Although metal knifes were common, the ritual had to be performed with a stone knife. There were so many flint implements to be found at the surface of Palestine in the Iron Age, that it is likely that the very fine neolithic flints were often picked up and used for certain purposes. The art of making such fine tools was however already long lost.

The casual use of unfashioned stone is enormous, and stone objects

---

[1]) cf. p. 160.

on which the very minimum work has been done are usually put down by the exasperated archaelogist as : tethering stones, loom weights, door jambs. Life in a present-day Near-East village is most revealing in showing the inventive use to which unshaped pebbles and stones are used, even to the extent of jamming a wobbly head lamp on a bonnet or in place of more orthodox weights in a shop.

WEIGHTS

Literature:
Lachish III p. 348-56

Fifty eight stone weights were recovered from the Iron Age levels at at Lachish, six of which were inscribed with Early Hebrew letters and twelve with numerical or metrological signs Pl. XII. The stratigraphical evidence of the archaeological context in which they were found is not sufficiently clear to be able to ascribe any of these weights to a definite time limit. "Most of the weights were not associated with any particular building...no specimens inscribed with Hebrew words were found in tell rooms." But there was a small group which can probably be assigned to the post-Exilic re-occupation of the site. Otherwise "on epigraphic and archaeological grounds, it is impossible to assign exact dates to the weights". However, by a comparison of the script of the royal jar handles [1]) with that of the weights, a tentative seventh/sixth century B.C. date may be given.

The weights are mostly dome shaped, and made from relatively hard limestone. The inscribed weights bear the word *'neseph' 'pim'* or *'beqa' '* but "there are not two Early Hebrew specimens bearing the same inscription which have exactly the same weight". By a table of weights found at ten different sites in Palestine, Miss Tufnell proves her point, showing that there were even weights which were heavier than the average. "The Early Hebrew system of weights was thus far more complicated than had been supposed. We must assume that there were independant systems which probably varied according to the goods for sale, just as nowadays the chemist, the grocer and the jeweller use different standards; and that also these systems varied locally. We have it on the authority of the Bible that the *beqa'* (the only weight known from the Bible of which examples have survived) was used for weighing gold (Genesis xxiv: 22), that it was the poll tax (Exodus xxxviii : 26) and that it was 'half a sheqel according to the sheqel of the sanctuary', i.e. half of the 'sacred' sheqel....A

---

[1]) P. W Lapp: *B.A.S.O.R.* no. 158. p. 14.

standard metrological system of early Palestine has yet to be discovered, if, indeed, it ever existed". (*o.c.*, p. 350)

A DYE-PLANT FROM TELL BEIT MIRSIM

Literature:

Tell Beit Mirsim III. A.A.S.O.R., XXI-XXII, pp. 56f.

At Tell Beit Mirsim a number of dye-plants were excavated, belonging to the last phase of Stratum A, which ended 589 B.C. The find of two of them is described by Albright as follows:

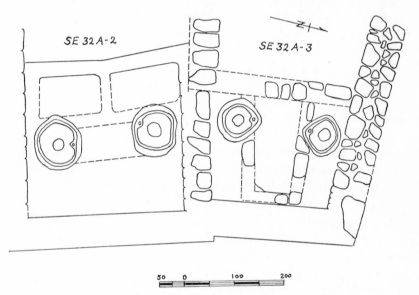

Fig. 52.   Ground plan of seventh century dye plants in SE 32 A,
Tell Beit Mirsim.

"The most important dye-plants were two built side by side, with two round stone vats in each". Cf. fig. 52 and Pl. XIII. "The vats themselves were surprisingly uniform in size and form. All varied between 70 and 90 cm in height and diameter, and all contained a relatively small and roughly spherical basin, between 30 and 45 cm in diameter, with a mouth one-half to two-thirds as wide. Around the rim of all four vats was chiseled a circular groove, obviously to catch the dye, which ran back into the vat through a connecting hole. When the dye was being stirred up a small stone was inserted into the hole from outside, in order to keep the liquid from splashing out. Several of these stones were found still in place as we excavated in different dye-plants. In room 2 there were two solidly constructed rectangular basins of stone and plaster just in front of the basins, together with a bench between the latter; the basins were about 65 cm. deep and averaged about 1.30 m in length and 0.90 in width. In room 3 there was a narrow bench in front of the two vats and a rectangular basin of stone and mortar (partly plastered) between them; the basin measures about 1.80 by 0.80 m and was about 55 cm. deep. Between the vats in room 2 was a large handleless jar S.N. 247, set in the bench already mentioned. This jar was nearly the same shape as the two jars published TBM I, Pl. 52: 12-13, but was somewhat larger (51-35 cm); since the first of the two jars was employed as a dye-vat set in a stone bench in NW 42A-2, the point is important. In room 2 there were three wall-cupboards and in room 3 there were two more. In the two corners of room 2 nearest the vats were found standing upright the two hole-mouth jars S.N. 248 and 249, while in the same positions in room 3 stood the hole-mouth jars S.N. 250 and 251. At least two of the hole-mouth jars were partly full of slaked lime. One of them was covered with a flat stone when found. Since we found two exactly similar jars in precisely the same positions in dye-plant SE 23A-10, we are again confronted with a standard pattern. In room 3 were found at least six large perforated stones, like the stones found in other dye-plants in the site. There may have been more, but we could not remove them without endangering the stability of the badly sagging north wall... At the other end of room 3, away from the vats, was a long, masonry bench, originally about 2.20 m long and 0.55 wide, on which was some pottery, including a large two-handled pitcher. When the rooms were excavated they were found to be full of a solid mass of calcined stone, lime, plaster and brick, which was nearly as hard as concrete, indicating a terrific conflagration at the time of the final destruction of the town in cir. 589 B.C."

Further dye-plants of Str. A are described in par. 37. In par. 37 follows the study of comparative material, including an interesting account of the technique of dyeing in Palestine [1]). Albright gives a wealth of literature concerning the subject and many suggestions of possible explanations. The finds are catalogued but only a few are published.

The dye-plants from Tell Beit Mirsim belong to the best preserved

---

[1]) cf. Dalmann, *Arbeit und Sitte in Palestina* V, pp. 77f.

workshops from the Iron Age. Traces of various other types of workshops have been found, and of metal industries. Recently more information has been recovered concerning the wine trade and a wine-making centre has been excavated at el-Gib, as yet mentioned only in preliminary reports, since the excavations are still in progress. Shechem, Hebron and Gibeon were all important wine centres. Stamped jar handles bearing the name of the city and sometimes the name of the maker have been found in other Palestinian cities: for instance products from Hebron have been found in Lachish and Hazor. Whether much wine was exported abroad is unknown, but seems likely. The lower riverlands of Egypt and Mesopotamia were not suitable for vineyards and olive groves and it is very likely that they relied on these Palestinian products. The only reference in the Bible to export of wine concerns Tyre trading with Damascus: "Damascus was thy merchant in the multitude of thy wares, of thy making..in the wine of Helbon and white wool", Ezech. xxvii 18.

Similarly traces have been found of olive oil making at Tell Beit Mirsim, a weaver's establishment (Lachish) and small metal industries (Shechem, Sellin's excavations and probably Iron Age.) The reader is referred to the excavation reports and general studies for further information. Here we have dealt with a few aspects of daily work in ancient Israel, the work of the potter, best known to us, work with stone, to show the many possibilities of use in Iron Age society, and the dye-plant, one of the best preserved workshops where vegetable material was used. Judging from the skill of the Israelite potter we may assume that other craftsmen turned out equally serviceable products.

CHAPTER SEVEN

MATERIAL REMAINS AND SPIRITUAL LIFE

What really is the purpose of excavation in Biblical sites to-day? The answer is not so straightforward as it might seem, but an attempt will be made here to provide it and to suggest channels into which some of the extensive archaeological activies in Palestine to-day might be diverted.

Archaeology in general must be considered first and foremost as the handmaid of history, and the ordinary accepted methods of deducing and assessing what is historical must be used. A confessional or 'marxist' interpretation of archaeology is quite unacceptable.

Without archaeology we could disprove Archbishop Usher's date for the creation of the world, but we could not say, as we now can at least in part, how man lived in 4002 B.C. Without archaeology the historical presence of such civilizations as that of the Hittites or Hurrians of Mari would be quite unknown to-day.

Along with factual historical data, Near Eastern expeditions in the past have filled the museums of the world with such wonders of the ancient world as the Ram-in-the-thicket from Ur and the Nimrud ivories. They have provided philologists not only with the key to the decipherment of ancient languages, but have also provided them with whole libraries of texts from such different sources as el-Amarna, Ras Shamra, Nuzi, Mari, etc. Ugaritic and Hurrian are two languages with an advanced literature which were totally unknown before the days of archaeological expeditions.

All this activity in and around the Fertile Crescent has resulted in the traditional position of the Biblical texts being challenged. The Old Testament now has other contemporary literature with which it can be compared both linguistically, and as to content. The historical events described in the O.T. can in general be dovetailed into the complex pattern of Iron Age history in the Near East. It is even possible to provide a background to certain O.T. figures. We can point to the type of house Amos might have lived in, the sort of water jar he could have drunk from. What the O.T. has lost in uniqueness, it has gained in actuality. By achieving a truely historical setting, it has become far more tangible.

With all this to their credit, what are archaeologists after to-day?

Unfortunately there is no general plan among the many different groups working in Jordan and Israel to-day. One thing can safely be said: they are no longer digging with the object of finding artistic objects suitable for their museum showcases. On the other hand the recovery of texts has been much stimulated by the chance finds of the Dead Sea Scrolls. The romance and commercialism surrounding this sort of work has attracted and dispirited various types of excavators. The present political set-up in Palestine has also naturally influenced archaeological policy: new states understandably want to demonstrate that their people's roots have been long in the ground they now possess. A further trend has been to concentrate on the pre-history of Palestine rather than O.T. times, not only because it covers such an important and exciting part of man's development, but also because it saves the archaeologist all the laborious problems of trying to fit archaeological and Biblical evidence together without either loosing professional integrity or giving offence to colleagues.

Broadly speaking one can compare the stage at which Palestinian archaeology has arrived with that of social anthropology when it was typified by Fraser's Golden Bough. This phase was devoted to the analysis of culture traits without reference to the cultures as an integrated whole. Archaeology in Palestine has reached a stage which its participators can look back at the romantic era and the time when Biblical confirmation was so desparately sought after. Work as a whole there is gradually getting onto a professional footing, and the way is open for various possible developments. The danger is that more and more non-integrated facts may emerge, leading to sterile historical, cultural and religious interpretation.

The work of three major English archaeologists in the Palestinian field can perhaps best illustrate this development. Petrie with his almost miraculous flair for giving the right historical answer based on the minimum of factual evidence, set Palestine squarely on the ancient historical map. Garstang, with far more O.T. knowledge and greater academic resources than Petrie, deepened our knowledge of Palestinian cultures and brought them into closer contact with the neighbouring countries. But his orthodox faith caused him to leap to conclusions which were sometimes less historically exact than Petrie's freer imagination. Miss Kenyon has put disciplined technical methods into practise in an area which is in crying need of exact, factual, statistical attention.

Enormous quantities of unrelated or partially related cultural, social and religious information have been excavated. It has been interpreted in the light of O.T. texts and ancient written sources from neighbouring countries. Objects and situations have been compared and contrasted and a passably coherent cultural picture has been formed, in which a great number of hypotheses await confirmation or denial. In all probability the main historical and cultural lines that have been drawn up in the past half century will long remain valid. The time has now come when the archaeologists ought to busy themselves with these hypotheses, and though of necessity excavators deal with material rather than spiritual evidence, there is no reason why a minutely detailed study of certain material remains should not yield evidence of certain spiritual traits, practices or taboos.

It cannot be too strongly stressed that such conclusions can only be drawn from objects properly excavated and attributed to their correct strata, and only in conjunction with their context as a whole. To illustrate this contention, two types of finds—both common in Iron Age sites—have been chosen here: terracotta figurines and animal bones.

TERRACOTTA FIGURINES

Terracotta figurines representing both humans and animals, have been found in every Iron Age site yet excavated. They appear in various distinctive styles both mass produced from moulds and hand formed individually. The interpretation of these figurines remains fluid. In general they are said to be votive offerings or manifestations of sympathetic magic for fertility cults. The female figurines with their exaggerated sexual attributes are dubbed 'Astarte' goddesses or the dea nutrix, and the presence of these objects in Israelite cities is said to be confirmation of the backsliding of the people so frequently deplored by the prophets.

This general interpretation may well be correct as far as it goes. But without a single new figurine being found a study could be made which might alter or at least enlarge our knowledge of the use of these figurines. Here is a possibility of getting closer to the mind of Palestinian Iron Age man.

The lines on which this study might be drawn up are as follows:

1. Careful distinction between animal and human figurines, dealing with each group separately.

2. Statistical survey including:

   a) total number found;
   b) proportionate distribution geographically, and with regard to population figures where known;
   c) reliability of excavation in which found;
   d) where found, *i.e.* sanctuary, home, grave; Canaanite or Israelite area of land;
   e) whether they are restricted to certain social groups or widespread throughout the community;
   f) frequency in agricultural villages in comparison with trading cities;
   g) context in which they are found: is there any pattern in this context?
   h) are the different styles contemporary, overlapping, regional?

3. Comparison to Iron Age figurines found in Syria etc. after a similar statistical study had been worked out on those figurines.

Owing to the type of archaeology executed in Palestine for so long, this type of statistical survey will probably contain more query marks than factual information. But even this would be better than nothing. It might provide useful negative information and would show up the weak points in archaeological strategy, and where greater efforts ought to be made.

Two outstanding difficulties concerning the acceptance of the astarte/fertility theory must be mentioned. Why are the human figurines so different stylistically if they were indeed made for the same purpose? (cf. fig. 53 and Plates XIII b-XV).

Is the placid, curly headed, trumpet-shaped female figurine supporting heavy breasts on her folded arms really the image of the same imagination which formed the naked tambourine player, adorned in elaborate headdress, necklace and anklets? If one is the mother-goddess then the other is surely the priestess.

And why, if the animal figurines were modelled as fertility cult objects, are the animals never depicted as pregnant nor sexually exaggerated? Nor does the range of animals depicted cover the entire repertoire of known domesticated animals. It is significant that the great majority of fragments found belong to the horse and what can

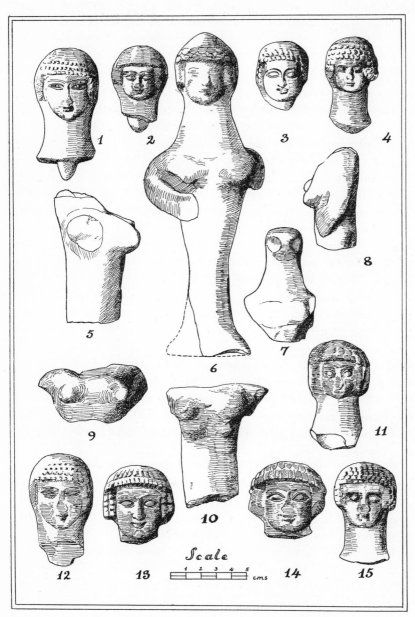

Fig. 53. Terracotta figurines from Tell Beit Mirsim.

be deduced from the fact that horse figurines in other lands are often associated with sun worship? (Pl. XVI and XVII a. b.).

ANIMAL BONES

The second subject is that of animal bones. Fragments of animal bones abound in any excavated site, and are generally the remains of meals, either profane or sacred. Various excavations have kept some sort of a record of the types of bones found, which have duly been identified and worked on in laboratoria after the field work was over. This is better than nothing, but of course far more cultural, social and religious information can be gained from a thorough study of the bones *in situ*, as is generally done on pre-historic excavations. The problem is touched at Lachish where various pig bones were found in a tomb dated by its contents to c. 900 B.C. 'overlaying a quantity of human remains...These had all been thrown in through the hole in the roof and no order was observable: juglet 171 was actually inside a skull' (*Lachish* III, 187)

Elsewhere (o.c., p. 64) it is recorded that: "it cannot be said that the animal bones were spread with deliberate intention to defile the human remains below; indeed the reasons for the deposit remain obscure," Dorothea Bate in her notes on the animal remains (*o.c.*, p. 410) remarks that "had the population..in those times been of Hebrew race it would have been curious to find the remains of pigs so plentiful." She accepted the opinion of one anthropologist who had studied the human crania from tombs at Lachish that the population was of Egyptian origin, a view which was challenged by another eminent anthropologist.

The whole problem of the interpretation of these pig bones is concentrated on the fact that there is not enough comparative material available. Nor is each link in the chain of evidence equally strong. Can we be sure that the pig skulls are a) contemporary with the rest of the tomb deposit, and b) if the human skulls in the tomb are said to be Egyptian, is there any reason to suppose that this is evidence pointing to a colony of traders living in Lachish? The pig was sacrificed to Osiris whose sacred animal he was. Many of the amulets found in Lachish are Egyptian in style, and one even represents the pig. All these separate pieces of information make it impossible to put the interesting suggestion that these bones indicate a break with the Deuteronomic food laws (and that this was the unspeakable sin of Lachish (Micah i: 11)) on a firmer footing. The fact that pig bones are found on other Iron Age sites can neither refute nor confirm it. It could be taken as an indication that the food taboos though vigorous in the capital never made themselves felt in outlying districts. It could even be that for certain feasts the taboo, unclean animal had to be sacrificed, typifying a well-recognised trait in anthropological studies, releasing what Ruth Benedict terms 'the Dionysian virtue that lies in the terrible and the forbidden' (*Patterns of Culture*, p. 165). All these suggestions must remain hypothetical until a more accurate and greater amount of information about animal remains is assembled.

However two remarkable facts about animal remains have been established at the excavation of the Fosse Temple at Lachish. They all represent young animals, mostly sheep or goat and practically all the recognizable bones are metacarpals of the right foreleg. This recalls the Mosaic peace offering of the right shoulder which was afterwards retained by the priest as his own. Near the altar of Structure I a large number of knuckle bones were found, which by analogy with Babylonian custom could witness to the fact that all knuckles of lambs and cattle were reserved for the priest. So here is evidence of a Canaanite ritual practise not so long before the arrival of the Israelites in the land. The tragedy is that in no other published excavation of a sanctuary in Palestine has similar attention been paid to the animal remains. Thus no comparable study is possible.

The presence or absense of pig bones in strata of the historical period could help the O.T. scholar to date the beginning of the food taboos, and thus help towards fixing the date of the written text.

These two features, the figurines and the animal bones, have been touched here in order to make it clear that just as the techniques of excavation have developed in such a way that the theologian is no longer competent to excavate a site without professional archaeologists, so is he no longer able to rely alone on his linguistic knowledge of the O.T. and its theology for the interpretation of the material remains of Iron Age man in Palestine. The bio-chemist with his pollen analysis to determine climatic changes and the physicist with C14 tests will play a less important role for the excavator of the historical period than for the pre-historian. But if the material remains are ever going to throw light on cultural and spiritual areas of knowledge, then the social anthropologist, the statistician, osteologist, etc must be given a much larger (and preferably on the spot) share of the initial interpretation of finds.

Is the O.T. scholar then to be confined to literary interpretation and exegesis? On the contrary, all the results, both negative and positive, produced by the specialist cannot hope to form a coherent picture until the O.T. scholar has reviewed them in the light of his literary knowledge of the Bible, study of primitive and comparative religions etc, and linked the several threads into an integrated whole.

It has been shown how two specialized subjects might be handled to extract more meaning and, en passant, supply more information concerning the religious thought of ancient Israel. A background to the life of ancient Israel ought also to provide a background to the thought of the times. For that reason alone all accurate and careful excavation done in Palestine is welcome, even if it appears disjointed and scrappy, provided more collation and integration is done on the material produced than is at present the general case. The great advantage is that the material evidence is contemporary with the soil it lies on. Its evidence is as unbiased as only an inanimate object can be. Its meaning has not been subjected to propaganda purposes, edited or incorrectly copied as textual evidence so frequently was. Apart from the changes wrought by time, both the material object and the situation in which it is found are recovered as they were left in antiquity. The material is authentic but also anonymous. This is an important limitation. Even if we could visit Madame Tussaud and see the authentic hat which Napoleon wore at Waterloo, it would be filled by a waxen head and not the living flesh and bone of the Emperor himself. The image could never tell us why the battle was lost, and that after all is what matters, not the authenticity of the hat. Just as the identity of the authors of some of the finest passages in the Bible will remain forever hiden, so the vast majority of the dwellers of Iron Age Palestine will never be more than a cipher in an excavation report. Here and there potter's marks scratched on the handles of their ware have been found, much as the medieval workman set his mark on the stones he laid. But individual names from seal stones or ostraca are extremely rare.

Though the individual person in antiquity remains unknown, his trades and professions can be differentiated, and as these occupations remain fairly consistant through the ages their development can be traced and general conclusions concerning the cultural and social scene can be made.

The potter's trade is the one which offers the greatest scope. Nothing short of the discovery of an ancient potter's manual (which would almost certainly never have existed) could ever have supplied the information we now have at our disposal about this profession except excavation. As it is we have the potter's workshop, probably nearly fully equiped, found at Lachish, potter's wheels from Hazor and other sites, and the evidence of his wares in every spadeful of earth turned over. The sherds which we find not only provide us with our basic chronology for historical events, trade influences and indications of material well-being or economic recession. They can also be analysed technically. A working potter to-day can demonstrate that a certain type of finish on a jug can only be achieved by turning the vessel on a wheel at a certain speed and working the surface with a particular tool held in a particular way. The chemist can reconstruct the temperature at which the ovens were fired, and the geologist can ascertain whether the clays used were locally quarried or brought from a distance. None of the facts alone would be of more than passing interest to a small body of specialists. But when taken in conjunction with each other they form a basis for broader studies, whose relevance to Biblical interpretation can readily be grasped.

For instance: do the techniques of Canaanite potters carry on unbroken far into the Israelite period? Are there signs of new techniques coming into use at the beginning of the Israelite occupation, or of an assimilation of techniques? [1]) If these questions could be satisfactorily answered then we would be well on the way to knowing whether the Israelites under Joshua were typical desert dwellers (*i.e.* without pottery) and whether they conquered the land or infiltrated over a longer period. In other words, were they immediately assimilated into Canaanite society, did they overthrow the social structure of Canaan straight a way, or did they form their own separate community amongst the Canaanites only gradually mixing with them? When one considers the innumerable works written on the problem of the Exodus and Settlement, it is astonishing to relate that no work has yet been published on the comparison and correlation of Dyn. 19 Egyptian Delta pottery forms and techniques with those of the earliest known Israelite pottery from Palestine. If a people had dwelt amongst foreigners even in slavery, for as long as a generation is it not highly possible that certain skilled techniques would be acquired and reproduced later in the home-land, however crudely?

---

[1]) It is remarkable that the Iron Age pottery almost completely looses the decoration with motifs from nature, and hardly shows any attempts to decorate pots at all.

Another outstanding problem is concerned with the decoration of pots. Painted pottery was very popular in the latter part of the L.B. age, and reached a high standard of bold, stylised patterns incorporating birds, geometric designs etc. before dropping off to the extremely decadent, slipshod liniar work of the E.I. age. In a world which almost certainly did not recognise art for art's sake, what was the underlying reason for this decoration and its decline?

As soon as certain material cultural traits or technical achievements can be ascribed to the Israelites which are alien to the Canaanites, then there is a chance that these two groups can be distinguished socially. If archaeologists ever succeed in doing this, then it will be up to the theologians to review and re-assess various religious questions in the light of this material evidence. The question of the Covenant and the dating of the Ten Commandments could be affected by this, just as much as the historical problems connected to the Settlement.

The very core of Israelite religion is expressed in the first commandment. This commandment does not seem to stand at the end of a long process of religious thought and development, but at the very beginning of the life of Israel in Palestine. It is due to the nature of the Old Testament writings that it is very difficult to conclude what influence this commandment had from the earliest times on the life of those tribes that accepted it by the Covenant. If we have to accept the complaint of the author of Judges that everybody in the early days did what seemed right in his eyes, then we simply cannot expect that archaeology will ever be able to contribute to the understanding of this central part of the 'creed'. If however on the other hand this verdict has to be taken as a sign of 'oriental despair' and exageration, then we ought to be able to work out in the long run the characteristic differences between the culture of the late Canaanites and the early Israelites, simply from the influence that the first commandment exercised on daily life. There is as yet very little archaeological evidence from undoubtedly early Israelite context, but it will remain one of the most important tasks of archaeology to provide the evidence.

Palestinian archaeology suffers from the masses of excavated material that cannot properly be evaluated by lack of precision in the excavator's techniques. As long as every object that presumably was a cult object but cannot be fitted into the cult of Jahwe can be taken as a Canaanite intrusion, Palestinian archaeology will not grow out of its romantic period, and it will remain of very little help to the student of the Bible. Instead of vagueness of interpretation, archaeology should turn out hard facts and statistical evidence exactly like a sociological study of economics in a poor mining district. Instead of turning to archaeological finds in cases where it suits the biblical student (often chance finds), Old Testament scholars should formulate their questions and urge the archaeologist to cooperate to find an answer. Thus the dating of the Late Bronze age city of Jericho as given by Miss Kenyon is not only of historical importance, it is, when the archaeological *situation* is taken into account, of first rate importance for the interpretation of the story of the fall of Jericho. And this would tell us a good deal about the mind of the author of the first chapters of the book of Joshua and his theological views.

All this illustrates the fact that Biblical archaeology still has many discoveries to make in the field where sure results are only obtained after long and strictly systematic research. It is also clear, however, from what has been said above, that evidence from the soil does provide us with scraps of information concerning spiritual life in antiquity. This information is probably the hardest to obtain but it is the most valuable information the soil can give us. This information can only be gained from purely factual evidence, systematically collected, firmly based on stratigraphy and statistically worked out.

In the following part of this chapter some archaeological evidence concerning the religious life of the Israelites is discussed. Unfortunately no precise archaeological information can be given either about the sanctuary of Jerusalem [1]) or of the state sanctuaries of the Northern Kingdom. No 'high places', mentioned frequently in the Old Testament, have as yet been excavated nor any of other sanctuaries that are connected with biblical history. One often finds a description of the so-called 'Conway High Place' at Petra quoted as a type of Canaanite sanctuary. It is possible that the stone structure built against the 'circular processional way around a sacred rock' at the south east side served as an altar but the rock-cut trench and the pavement are certainly nothing else but the remains of a corner tower of the pre-Roman defence wall of the city of Petra [2]). Various archaeological surveys have been made around Jericho to try and locate the ancient site of Gilgal. From the textual evidence of the Old Testament we know that this should be a Late Bronze Age sanctuary in the time of Joshua. The suggested sites all date from Iron Age II

[1]) See below.
[2]) *V.T.* Vol. XI 1961 p. 473.

or later. Moreover, since we cannot obtain a clear idea from the written sources what the nature of a 'gilgal' really is, archaeologists do not really know what to look for. Stone circles are frequently found and reported, dating from mesolithic times to those made today by mobile units of the army and the Beduin alike to protect their tents from wind.

At Megiddo a 'sacred area' was discovered which gave but slight indications of the Israelite cult in the early stages of the Kingdom. At Beth Shan two buildings dating from approximately the same period have been discovered and identified as sanctuaries. One is supposed to have been dedicated to Malkart, the Syrian God and the other to his female counterpart. Here we would have purely Canaanite sanctuaries in an Israelite context. Until the Iron Age strata to which these buildings belong have been published we will not know enough about the population to be able to draw far reaching conclusions from these two pagan sanctuaries. It remains to be seen whether the population changed after king David extended his power over the city. Megiddo presents a different case. The city lay bare for a long period during which the Israelite tribes settled in the country and was presumably rebuilt during the reign of king Solomon and then obviously settled by the Israelites. What has been found in this city in respect to the cult is shortly described below. The finds represent various classes of objects that are found in many excavations and often seem to be related to the cult. Two more classes of finds are described below in relation with the subject of this chapter. A short account is given of the ivories found at Samaria, originating from the 'ivory house' of the palace. And finally some tombs are discussed as tombs are generally an important source of knowledge about certain aspects of the spiritual life of a people.

From the three temples at Jerusalem, which were erected by Solomon, Zerubbabel and Herod the Great respectively, nothing has remained except the rock on which they stood. In and around the Old City of Jerusalem there are still many stones used by Herod for the building of his temple, robbed in early times as building material and incorporated in other buildings. A marble slab and a fragment of another have been found bearing the inscription which forbids foreigners to enter the inner courtyard [1]). Naturally it is the inscription which identifies the stone.

---

[1]) *Revue Archéologique*, XXIII, 1872, pp. 214-234; *Jewish Quarterly Review* XXXVII 1947, pp. 387-405.

It thus becomes clear that a reconstruction of the three buildings can only be done by study of comparative material and the literary sources. There is general agreement on the plan of the buildings, whereas questions like the ornaments and decoration remain difficult.

The first temple was built under supervision of Phoenician architects, and the third one undoubtedly under strong influence of Roman architecture. Phoenician art shows many foreign influences. Since king David started the planning of the erection of a royal sanctuary in Jerusalem, it is well possible that the Phoenician builders under king Solomon had to adapt their plans in certain details to drafts made to fit the needs of the cult of JHWH. This would make reconstruction of the building more uncertain and may well explain why no close parallels have been found yet. The temple of JHWH in Jerusalem is a special study and students are refered to the relevant literature [1]).

The proper study of the material remains of cults found in Israelite levels should be preceded by a thorough study of the biblical and non-biblical sources concerning both the cult of JHWH in its development throughout the ages and the cults of the Canaanites, as well as the partial fusion of both in the earlier stages. We know e.g. that the first temple of Jerusalem often, and from the early days of its existence, showed signs of the introduction of elements foreign to the cult of JHWH. Besides there is the interpretation of the cult of JHWH in the Northern Kingdom which tends to diverge from that in the Kingdom of Judah.

This makes it extremely difficult to decide whether an early sanctuary, in use before the centralisation of the cult in Jerusalem, was actually dedicated to the worship of JHWH. It is even often very uncertain, whether a certain building was a sanctuary or a building that served other purposes. Many of the so called sanctuaries of earlier excavation reports are clearly of a profane nature. Buildings with upright stones and the class of the so called 'Hilani' buildings [2]) have been treated as holy places. The same holds good for various objects which were considered part of the cult equipment from lack of a better explanation.

---

[1]) See e.g. J. Simons, *Jerusalem in the Old Testament*, Leiden, 1952. Ch. VI P. L. Garber, *Reconsidering the reconstruction of Solomon's Temple*, J.B.L., vol. LXXVII, 1958 pp. 123ff.

[2]) Notably at tell en-Nasbeh; Megiddo.

THE SACRED AREA OF MEGIDDO STR. V

This stratum was attributed by the excavators to E.I. (= 1200-1000 in their terminology), and presumably to the later part of this period. H. G. May points out [1] that the uncertainties about the stratigraphy are partly due to the history of its excavation. The excavators gave numbers of findspots to rooms only and objects found outside buildings could not be properly attributed to levels in their system. There seems to have been a gap in the occupation of the tell between the end of Str. VI and the beginning of Str. V whereas Str V is immediately followed by Str. IV [2]. The date of Str. V cannot be fixed with certainty since the attribution of the objects to the levels is not always certain and even the attribution of buildings to a stratum is sometimes doubtful. Since Str. V generally falls within the period after the Israelites had established themselves in most of the country it may be assumed that they rebuilt Megiddo after it had been deserted for more than a century. (No mention is made in the Bible of the capture of Megiddo during the Israelite conquest of the country.) In the eastern part of the tell, in area C many objects were found, which may have had some religious significance. May, believed one building, belonging to Str. IV, was a temple and fortress and two other buildings in Str. V are described as a 'building with upright stones' and 'a long storehouse'. May discusses the possibility that the upright stones were maṣṣeboth in a temple (p. 20) without committing himself to either possibility. The objects were found in several buildings and in the 'open spaces' between them. In view of the early date of Str. V in the history of the Israelites the suggestion of Miss Kenyon [3] that there may have been private chapels in individual houses is very interesting. The existence of such private chapels has not been proved from the plans of early Israelite levels.

THE OBJECTS

See Plates XVIII-XX.

A. *The upright stones.* Pl. XVIII. It is impossible to conclude from the published evidence concerning building 1A that it was a shrine. No significant objects were found in this building (*Meg.* I, p. 149).

---

[1] H. G. May, *Material Remains of the Megiddo Cult*, O.I.P. XXVI, Chicago, 1935, p. 4.
[2] See Kenyon Archaeology, p, 250.
[3] *o.c.*, p. 251.

B. *The proto Ionic Capitals.* They are probably dated too early in this Vol. (See *Samaria-Sebaste* I, p. 14) and are not a specific element of temple architecture (See May, *o.c.*, pp 39-42).

C. *Limestone altars.* Pl. XIX a. Small altars have been found in several excavations. They are thought to have been too small for animal sacrifices and it is suggested that they were incense burners. (*T.B.M.* XXI § 16)

D. *Pottery shrines.* The shrine (*o.c.* Pl xiii, shrine 2986, possibly Str. IV) has been hypothetically restored and only the general aspects of the shrine are represented. The walls rise above the level of the roof. The lower apertures in the front and sides represent windows and doors. It is suggested that the small circular openings above are pigeon holes for the sacred birds of the cult. A female sphinx is standing at each corner. This model shrine possibly served as an incense burner, as the inside face of the parts of walls projecting above the roof are discoloured by smoke. See May, p. 14 for some comparisons and literature. If it is indeed a model the object gives us a an impression of a real chapel and the way they were built. The cherub motif occurs also in the temple of king Solomon.

E. *Kernos ring.* Pl. XX b. This object is attributed to Str. VI (see o.c. p. 17 and pl. XVI) Fragments have been found on several sites, but the Megiddo example is well preserved.

F. *Censers.* Frontispiece. The ones published do not come from Str. V.

G. *Bronze stand.* Pl. XIX b. M. 1342 was originally published as found in Str. V but elsewhere it is stated that it was found by a shep herd on a dump. It has a square body and round neck. The four panels show a standing figure in front of a seated deity. The deity wears a long dress contrasting with the short skirt of the worshipper. In Cyprus stands were found on wheels, which makes a comparison with the bronze stands in the temple of Solomon possible. (see *o.c.*, p. 20)

H. *Pottery stands.* They have been frequently found in Palestine in connection with sanctuaries and the cult. (see *e.g. Lachish* II, *The Fosse temple*). The way they were used is not always clear yet. The examples from Megiddo date mainly from Str. VI.

I. *Pottery legs, phallus and rattle.* These objects again are found on many sites and they are apparently connected with cult-practises. The rattle, like the tambourine may have been used in processions, and the other objects may have served a magical purpose (healing or fertility). The rattle from Megiddo is unstratified.

J. *Pottery figurines. O.c.*, Pl. XXVI and XXVIII. M. 1454 is made in one piece in a mould. Traces of burnishing, fractured diadem of three horizontal bands, long braid terminating in coil over each breast, protuding pinhole eyes, pendant between the breasts on a necklace (?), no traces of arms.

M. 5418 is a 'pregnant mother goddess', yellow ware with red wash, right breast pierced, double incised line down the centre of body ending in volute, armlets, obscure girdle, anklets and collar. For a discussion see *o.c.*, Ch. IV. The Megiddo terracottas give a good impression of the various types found on I.A. sites in Palestine. They are generally thought to have been connected with fertility rites. The fact that the 'mother goddess' figurine was mass-produced and thus a cheap product indicates that they represent the nearest fertility powers or demons of the supernatural world, not necessarily the goddess Astarte. They have been found in all Israelite and Judaean levels, even in a royal palace of Judea[1]).

A great number of figurines was found in the Israelite shrine at Samaria[2]).

H. *Zoomorphic vessels.* Two were found in the 'sacred area' of Str. V. No. 3016 is reproduced here Pl. XVIII a. They are not necessarily connected with the cult. These types of vessels are fairly common on I.A. sites in Palestine.

The objects from the 'sacred area' from Megiddo, listed above and the parallels mentioned give a good impression of the material remains of a cult as found in the soil. It clearly shows that their place in the cult is often still obscure, and without the help of texts concerning the cults and more comparative material we cannot attempt to give a full explanation of their meaning and function.

IVORY CARVING FROM SAMARIA

Literature:

Samaria-Sebaste II: *Early Ivories from Samaria*; J. W. Crowfoot, and Grace M. Crowfoot; Palestine Exploration Fund, 1938.
Iraq II, 1935, p. 179-210 R. D. Barnett.
Bibliothèque archaéologique et historique, Tome XVI, 1931 *Arslan Tash*. F. Thureau-Dangin, etc.
The Monuments of Nineveh, Layard.

---

[1]) Ramet Rahel. I.L. N. 24 Dec. 1960, pp. 1140-'2
[2]) *S.S.* III p. 76ff.

In the debris of the Assyrian destruction of Samaria in 720 B.C. hundreds of ivory inlay fragments were recovered. The find spot lay between the great enclosure walls and the disturbance of this area is such that the ivories can not be assigned to any particular room or rooms.

Ivory was very common in Syria for centuries before and after the time of Ahab whose 'ivory house' (I Kings xxii 39) is one of his claims to fame. Phoenician traders seem to have been the centre of supply (I Kings x 22) and held not only this trade monopoly but also the monopoly of workmanship.

The ivories, Pl. XXI-XXIV which are most probably fragments of panelling and furniture inlay, (very few of them are carved in the round), can be divided into various catagories depending on subject matter, i.e. winged figures in human form, sphinx fragments, battling animals, a throned figure, the infant Horus, mythological subjects, patterns and borders and palm trees. Thus almost entirely of a religious or decorative order. Some carvings were further decorated by glass and paste insets in cloisonné work or overlaid with gold foil.

Though many of the plaques are superficially Egyptian in style or subject matter, not one can be said to be genuine Egyptian work. Ahab was married to Jezebel the Phoenician, but there is no reason to suppose that the Phoenician influence in the arts came into Palestine with her. In fact since the days of Solomon, Phoenicians had been employed by the rulers of Israel. As Crowfoot says: "The Egyptian trappings meant no more than the pseudo-classical draperies once thrown over Gospel characters in the West...they were a superficial dressing".

Two other collections of ivories, from Arslan Tash in Syria and Nimrud in Assyria, are contemporary both in date and style to those found at Samaria. A carved fragment from Arslan Tash was inscribed with the name of Hazael of Damascus who reigned in 840 BC, and ivories found in the palace of Sargon II by Layard in Nimrud were so un-Assyrian in style and so similar to those of Samaria that Miss Kenyon suggests that they could even be part of the loot from the sack of Samaria in 720 B.C. [1]). A further proof of the Phoenician craftsmanship of the Samaria ivories lies in the fact that a number of them had letters in the Hebrew—Phoenician script (the same script as that of the Hazael inscription) carved on their backs.

---

[1]) Ivory objects are frequently listed in Assyrian lists of tribute and spoil, *e.g.* they were offered by Hezekiah to Sennacherib in 701 B.C.

These letters are clearly not part of an inscription but were cut as guides to the joiner who had to assemble the plaques either on furniture or on a panel.

Whether the ivories were carved in Samaria or not is impossible to say, but the excavators are sure that the work was carried out by a single school of carvers and it is not unlikely that they were in fact made in the royal capital. Crowfoot (op. cit. p. 52-3) remarks on the similarity of decoration and repertoire, if on a different scale, used in Solomon's temple at Jerusalem to these ivories. "These...were made by Phoenicians, but they were made for the house of the Lord to the order of the king...The ivories at Samaria were carved similarly to the order of the king of Israel. Jewish tradition represents Solomon and Ahab as back sliders but similar breaches of the Mosaic law were committed by those who decorated the ark (Ex. xxv 20) and by the priestly Ezekiel (Ez. xii: 18) At this time Jahwism was not hostile to representational art".

Be that as it may, these ivories represent the taste and luxury of an absolute monarch of 8th century Israel. They reveal a derivative but delicate and true art which was imported from Phoenicia both because this art form was clearly fashionable in the great states round the Fertile Crescent at that time, and also because there was no stimulous through a wealthy aristocracy or from religious cults for an indigenous art form to take its place.

THE STUDY OF IRON AGE TOMBS

Archaeology has greatly increased its knowledge of early cultures by the excavation of graves and tombs. From a mere collecting of grave goods, archaeology has proceeded not only to the study of the finds, including the skeletons, but also to the study of the grave or tomb itself, its plan and construction and many aspects related to this. It has become clear that graves can tell an important story about the cultural achievements and the religious beliefs of the people that were buried in them. Provided enough graves or tombs of a certain culture are discovered and properly excavated, indispensible information about that culture is obtained. Hence the I.A. tombs in Palestine are of great importance to the student of Biblical archaeology.

For the beginner, the study of the tombs published in the excavation reports is the best introduction to the study of the excavated site.

Graves, dug in the sand or in clay are usually not 'reused', but rock-cut tombs often are. Chambers, cut into solid rock are often reused from Chalcolithic times onwards by people of different ages, who cleared out the contents before using them to bury their own dead. Stray sherds from earlier cultures prove to the archaeologist that the cave or chamber was 're-used'. Sometimes those stray sherds are only found in the entrance or shaft of the tomb. Rock-cut tombs of the I.A. may have been in use by a family for some centuries and in those cases the contents range over a long period of development of shapes. Hence the study should start from tombs that obviously were used for a short time only, and contain homogeneous pottery groups. These pottery groups can be reconstructed from the publication, and are in recent reports often published as groups together. Grave goods have usually suffered much less from destructive agents and are often undamaged. From these smaller groups a picture can be drawn of the development of the pottery of the I.A., which is an important aid in the reconstruction and redating of the strata of sites excavated in earlier days.

In contrast to the tombs of some other contemporary cultures, the I.A. graves and tombs from Palestine are as a rule devoid of any inscribed material and thus anonymous. Another drawback with respect to the tombs has been that the cemetries of various important towns with a numerous population during the I.A. have until now escaped detection by the archaeologists who excavated at those sites. Although often a small group or groups of tombs are found e.g. in the slopes of the tell or further away, large cemetries that date from the I.A. have not been discovered in spite of intensive search. At Jericho over 1100 tombs were found, dating from the earlier periods, but very few belonged to the city of the I.A. Similarly Samaria, Jerusalem, Shechem [1] tell el-Far'a, Beth Shan, tell en-Nasbeh, Tell Beit Mirsim and Megiddo have not given up the secret of the location of the I.A. cemetries. Sometimes a cemetry is found by chance. In 1924 P.L.O. Guy published [2] rock-cut tombs found at approximately 1 km distance from the nearest tell, Tell Abu Hawam, and in 1952 E. Anati found again at a distance of approximately 1 km from the same tell a number of individual burials in the sand. In a space of 20-12 m no less than 11 graves of the L.B.A. were excavated and it was established that the cemetry had extended

---

[1]) cf. *B.A.S.O.R.*, no 161, 1961 p. 16.
[2]) cf. *B.B.S.A.J.* 5, 1924 pp. 47ff.

originally over an area of over 200 hectares, most of the graves being eroded away now [1]).

As a result of this situation we know in fact very little about Israelite burials and burial customs, at least we have as yet little evidence for distinguishing Canaanite burials from Israelite burials. The importance of this will be shown in the discussion of the 'Israelite' tombs from Samaria. The amount of information that can be derived from the study of the finds from large cemeteries of different cultures and times can be judged from the results of the recent excavations at Jericho [2]). From the grave goods (or lack of grave goods) much can be deduced both about the culture of those living in that period, as well as about their religious beliefs, provided the total amount of excavated graves is big enough to allow for conclusions to be drawn.

LACHISH, TOMB 6006

The following is an example for the study of tomb groups. Tomb 6006 from Lachish [3]) is a rock cut tomb with a dromos and one chamber. The tomb was partly filled with earth. It was entered from the east [4]). The dromos was closed with neatly packed stones. Three steps led down to a doorway and inside the tomb chamber two more steps lead down to the floor of the chamber. On the west and the north were rock benches and above the bench to the right of the entrance was a niche with a lamp. A female skeleton was found on the western bench, and a male skeleton on the other bench. On the floor were found an iron knife and a storage jar (fig. 55 no. 476) 5 flasks of three different types were found near the head of the female skeleton, (fig. 55 nos. 315, 324, 329) and a bowl and a chalice were found near the male skeleton (fig. 55 nos. 15, 154) For the plan of the tomb cf. fig. 54. The tomb is dated c. 875 B.C. The development of the shapes of tombs from the Iron Age is discussed by Miss Tufnell o.c. pp. 174 ff. Apart from rock cut tombs a number of single graves were also found at Lachish, all dating from the early Iron Age.

---

[1]) cf. *ʿAtiqot* Vol. II, pp. 89ff.
[2]) cf. *Jericho* The Tombs, Vols. I and II.
[3]) cf. *Lachish* III Text. p. 247 and plan p. 248.
[4]) cf. *Lachish* III Plates. pl. 129 and Pl. 10, 52.

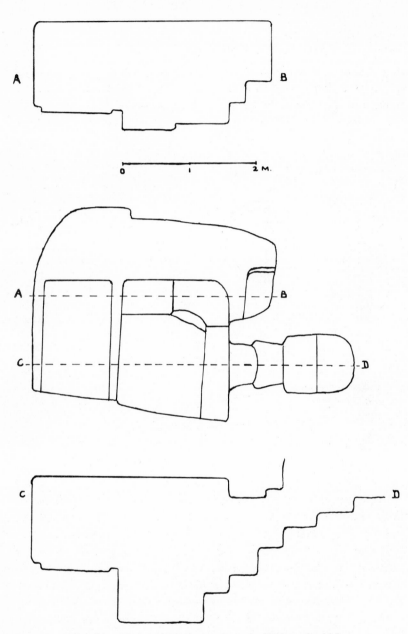

Fig. 54. Plan and sections of tomb 6006 at Lachish.

A GROUP OF ISRAELITE TOMBS FROM SAMARIA

Literature:

Samaria-Sebaste I pp. 21f (E. L. Sukenik).
Samaria-Sebaste III, p. 136 and 196ff.

The best preserved and most complete tomb, No. 103, of this group is at the north end of the area. It is an irregular cave measuring some 5 m. by 4.70 m. In the centre are remains of a rock pillar which once carried the roof of the cave but which has now collapsed.

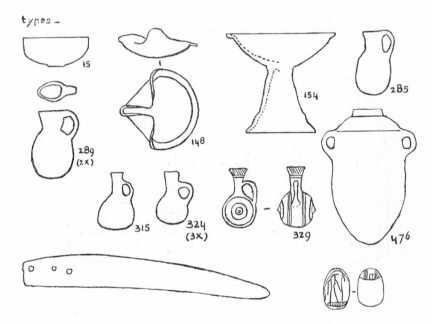

Fig. 55.   Pottery and objects from tomb 6006 Lachish.

An opening in the north wall led into a chamber 2.4 m. wide, 1.90 m. deep and 1.55 m. high, on about the same level as the cave. This chamber was identified as the burial place proper because it contained four skeletons; three adults and a child with their heads to the east. Outside the chamber, to the west, cut in the rock was a kind of bench, 0.44 m high. In the floor of the cave were six holes, some with a double rimmed mouth to carry a cover stone. Two of them were connected by a narrow, shallow channel. These holes opened into bottle-shaped rock-cut pits, varying in depth from 2.20 m to 4.50 m., and their lower diameter was from 1.80 m. to 2.90 m. The pits were full of pottery, much of which had apparently been broken intentio-

nally. They also contained bronze, iron, stone and bone objects, as
well as some animal bones identified by J. Aharoni as belonging to
an ass and a sheep or goat. There were no human bones.

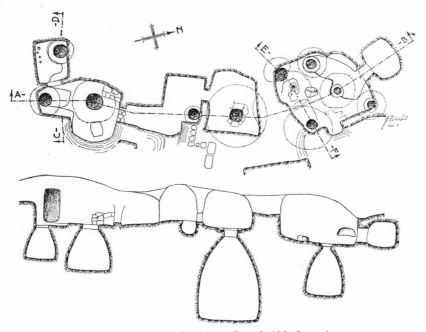

Fig. 56. Plan and section of tomb 103, Samaria.

Other tombs in this group were destroyed down to floor levels,
and only the pits remained.

Sukenik remarks: "The pits in the tomb-caves are to be explained
as the receptacles of offerings connected with the cult of the dead as
regularly practised in ancient Israel in spite of the attacks of the
prophets".

The excavators attribute these tombs to Period V at Samaria, at
the end of the 8th century B.C. The pottery from No. 103 is reproduced on fig. 57-'9 and other objects on fig. 60.

Some criticism of this interpretation is set out below. Sukenik
assumes that this tomb group is definitely Israelite in character, and
indeed the pottery found in this group of tombs is typical for Samaria,
the capital city. Without doubt, too, the pits were used as receptacles
for offerings, but they are a feature which does not appear in other
tombs of the period, which also contain grave goods. Why, if these

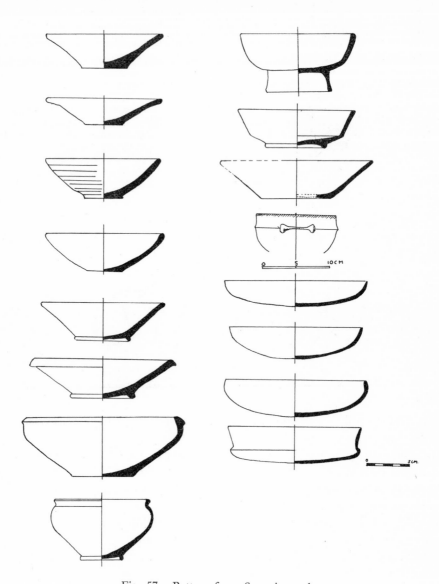

Fig. 57. Pottery from Samaria tombs.

graves are definitely Israelite, and the "cult of the dead was regularly
practised" by the Israelites, does this group contain an important
feature (the offering pits) which does not occur in any con-

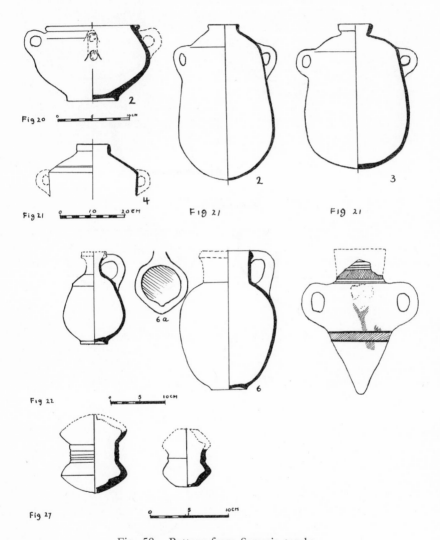

Fig. 58. Pottery from Samaria tombs.

temporary graves? This assumption that tombs found in Samaria
must belong to Israelites is further weakened when one recalls
that Samaria was a most cosmopolitan city at that time, having

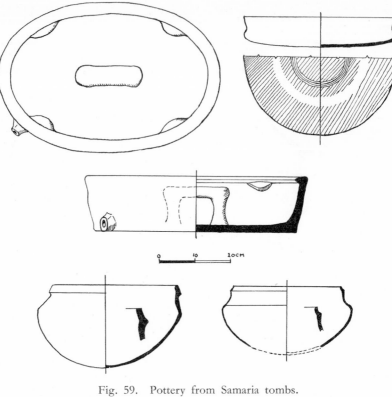

Fig. 59.   Pottery from Samaria tombs.

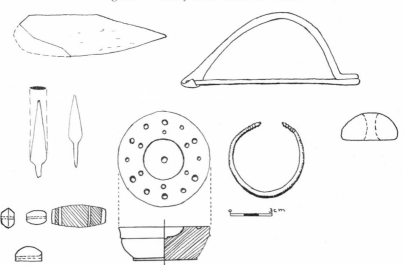

Fig. 60.   Objects from Samaria tomb 103.

among other groups, many traders from Damascus as part of the population [1]).

While there is equally well no proof for these tombs belonging to foreign elements in the city, it is surely no less uncertain that they belonged to Israelites.

No terracotta figurines are found in this group of graves, and from what is known in the O.T. about the ancient Israelite conception of death, one would not expect such fertility symbols in orthodox graves. This fact however does not bring us any nearer a firmer interpretation of ownership of these burials. A clue to the interpretation may lie hidden in the fact that these pits were not only used for pouring libations into, but the vessel itself was also thrown in. But one well-preserved and several fragmentary tombs of a certain type offers too little material on its own for a hard and fast assignment of ownership. The interpretation of this tomb group offers a fair example of the frustrations and limitations of Palestinian archaeology at its present stage.

---

[1]) *S.S.* I, p 1.

SHORT GLOSSARY

baulk (Am. *catwalk*) a strip of earth, generally a metre wide, left unexcavated across the excavation area. As work progresses on both sides of it, the sides of the baulk reveal pictorially the successive strata which have gone to make up the ancient site and serve as a check for stratigraphical digging. cf. *section*

beaker elongated drinking cup, usually without handle.

burnish a smooth sheen on the surface of a pot, achieved by sealing the surface pores of the leather-hard clay by pressing them with a pebble or bone tool. Hand-burnishing, with the pot held in the hand produces:

    continuous burnishing (short, close together going in all directions),
    ring burnishing (lines concentric with the rim)
    vertical burnishing
    radial burnishing
    various pattern designs

Wheel-burnishing, as the vessel spins on a very slow wheel, produces horizontal or spiral burnishing.

base, button base of pot ending in a small convex knob

—, *disk* convex base raised on ring

—, *ring* base formed on low ring

—, *string-cut* flat base bearing traces of having been cut off the lump of clay from which the vessel was made, with a piece of string.

base-ring ware Cypriot Late Bronze Age ware often imported into Palestine at that period. Hard, metallic ware with ring-base.

bilbil Cypriot jug made from base-ring ware.

caliciform Another term for Albright's MB1 (Middle Bronze 1) and Miss Kenyon's EB-MB (Intermediary Early Bronze-Middle Bronze Age).

carinated keel or ridge shaped. Typical for the sharp coutours of many MB forms.

chronology science of computing dates.

    absolute chronology: arrangement of events with fixed dates in history.
    relative chronology: arrangement of events successively in approximate historical periods.

dipper juglet small jug, usually with one handle, used for dipping into large storage jars and bringing out the liquid.

dump the pile of earth removed from the excavated area. Also known as the spoil heap.

handle, bar horizontal handle applied just below rim of bowl, frequent in the Iron Age.

—, *ledge* horizontal handle made from pinching up the clay from the wall of the vessel before firing. Frequent in EB and EB-MB forms.

—, *loop* normally placed perpendicularly, not horizontally, from lip to shoulder or neck.

—, *lug*: usually only on vessels which were meant to be suspended

—, *wish-bone*: in the shape of a wish-bone, these handles occur on Cypriot imports or on local imitations of them.

hole-mouth jar: large storage jar, the rim of which ends abruptly without growing out of a neck. Typical for the EB period.

pilgrim-flask: lentiod flask common in LB and Early Iron, with two loop handles on the neck apparently for tying the vessel to a shepherd's belt.

quern: hand mill for grinding corn.

section: a) The vertical cut made in a mound or ancient site; the sides of the area under excavation.

b) The drawing made of these sides or the sides of baulks, to represent the internal structure of the site through the superimposed levels of earth.

stratigraphy: science of measuring the successive strata of a site by pealing off the natural accumulation of earth layers in their original order.

stratum: ⎰
strata: ⎱ layer or set of successive layers of any deposited substance.

typology: system of compiling collections of similar objects to show development of form and style through a given period of time, and thus to arrive at a positive statement that one object of a type is older or younger than another.

tombs: always rock-cut or found in caves; generally they hold multiple burials, though single burials are also found. *Graves* are always shallow burials in the earth, generally single, though sometimes multiple.

ware: *hard* ware is when the sherd or vessel gives off a more or less metallic sound when taped with the finger, and when a scratch by the finger nail leaves no mark on the surface.

soft ware: when the sherd or vessel is of a more biscuit-like consistancy; when it does not sound metallic; and when it is easy to leave a mark on the surface.

fine ware: when the walls of the vessel are thin, hard and well finished.

coarse ware: when the clay of the vessel is mixed with much grit and straw; is heavy with thick walls.

well-levigated: when the grits in the clay are evenly distributed over the whole vessel.

well-fired: when the walls of a vessel are fired the same colour all the way through If the colour of a vessel is patchy, it is said to be *unevenly* fired.

wet-smoothed: when no slip or wash is applied but the vessel's surface is smoothed off by a tool when still leather hard. This removes the surface clay from the vessel.

slip: liquid clay about the consistancy of cream applied to a vessel either by being poured or brushed on; the vessel can also be dipped in. Several coats are applied at the leather-hard stage and then fired. A very common decoration.

wash: same as slip, but is applied after firing, and is never re-fired.

White Slip I and II: Cypriot pottery of the LB, sometimes imported into Palestine. Very fine ware with thick smooth white slip, and decorated in ladder patterns in orange/brown or black. A popular form is the milk bowl with wish-bone handle.

ENGLISH-FRENCH GLOSSARY

baulk	banquette
beaker	gobelet
burnish	lustré
base, button	base, en touton
disk	en disque
string-cut	coupée a la ficelle
base-ring ware	céramique à base en anneau
caliciform	caliciforme
carinated	caréné
dipper juglet	puisette
handle, bar	anse, en barre
ledge	horizontale
lug	oreillette
wish-bone	en triangle évidé
hole-mouth jar	jarre à large piverture sans col
pilgrim flask	gourde de pélerin
section	section
ware, fine	céramique, fine
well-levigated	bien épurée
well-fired	bien cuite
wet-smoothed	lissée
slip	engobe
wash	couverte
White Slip ware	céramique à engobe blanc
bilbil	bilbil

APPENDIX

Collections of Palestinian Excavation Material

There are various collections of Palestinian pottery and other objects, as well as study collections, in universities and museums all over the world. Here is a list of those best known to the authors.

Israel

The Hebrew University, Jerusalem.

Jordan

The Palestine Museum, Jerusalem (certainly the finest collection in the world, with exceptionally good study facilities)

The Museum, Amman.

England and *Scotland*

Birmingham, The Museum

Cambridge, The Fitzwilliam Museum

Durham, The University Museum

London, The Institute of Archaeology, Gordon Sq. W1 (an extremely large, well catalogued and accessible collection, comprising material from all the most important British led excavations in Palestine since the days of Petrie)

Oxford, The Ashmolean Museum

St. Andrews, University collection

Australia

Sidney, The University

Canada

Toronto, The Royal Ontario Museum

The Netherlands

Leiden, The Palestinian work rooms, Leiden University

— , Rijksmuseum van Oudheden

The United States

Baltimore, The Johns Hopkins University

Philadelphia, The University of Pennsylvania

Pittsburg, The Xenia Theological Seminary

Chicago, Drew University and McCormick Theological Seminary
        The Oriental Institute

California, Pacific School of Religion, Berkeley.

INDEX

BIBLICAL REFERENCES

PLATE I

C. H. Warren

Ch. Clermont-Ganneau

C. R. Conder

PLATE II

The wadi bed cutting through the mound at Tell el-Hesi showing some strata lines.

PLATE III

Section showing the plastered scarp of the MB age defences at Jericho.

Plate IV

Pit containing undisturbed Chalcolithic and EB levels.

PLATE V

Excavation with the aid of baulks in a conventional grid system.

Plate VI

But here walls are laid bare in their total length without any cross baulks to serve as checks on stratigraphy

PLATE VII

A. Hazor 1955

B. Samaria

,,Is there a general impression of clean, tidy work ?"

PLATE VIII

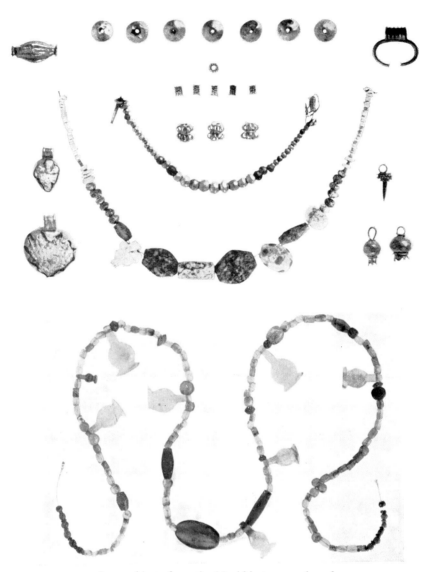

Some objects from the Megiddo treasure hoard.

PLATE IX

The equipment of a potter's workshop, Lachish.

PLATE X

The equipment of a potter's workshop, Lachish

PLATE XI

a. Basalt quern and grinder, from Iron Age, Deir ʿAllā

b. Delicate alabastron with incised decoration from Iron Age, Deir ʿAllā

PLATE XII

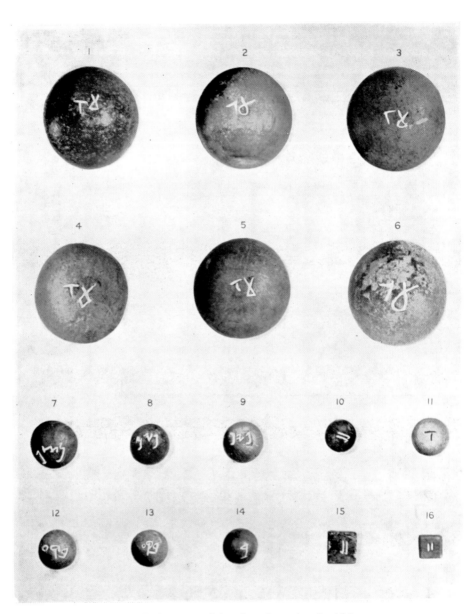

Inscribed stone weights from Iron Age Lachish.

PLATE XIII

A. Dye-plant from Tell Beit Mirsim. Iron Age

B. Astarte plaques from Bronze Age, Lachish

PLATE XIV

Iron Age figurines from Deir ʿAllā

A. Terracotta figurine: priestess with tamburine?

B. Two male terracotta figurines

PLATE XV

Iron Age figurines from Deir ʿAllā

A. Terracotta figurine heads with elaborate headdresses

B. Mould for a similar head

PLATE XVI

Animal terracotta figurines from Megiddo

PLATE XVII

A. Terracotta model of horse and rider. Lachish

B. Terracotta figurine of monkey with child, Iron Age Deir ʿAllā

PLATE XVIII

Building with upright stones from the sacred area, Megidda

PLATE XIX

A. A line stone altar. Megiddo.

B. Bronze offering stand, Megiddo.

PLATE XX

A. Zoomorphic vessel, Megiddo

B. Kernos ring, Megiddo

PLATE XXI

Carved ivories from Samaria

PLATE XXII

Carved ivories from Samaria

PLATE XXIII

Carved ivories from Samaria

PLATE XXIV

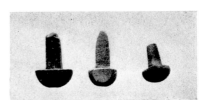

Carved ivories from Samaria

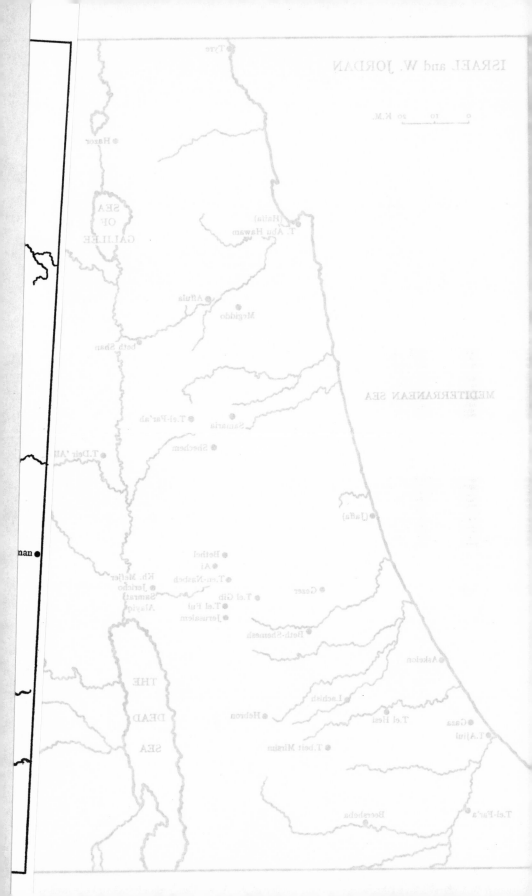

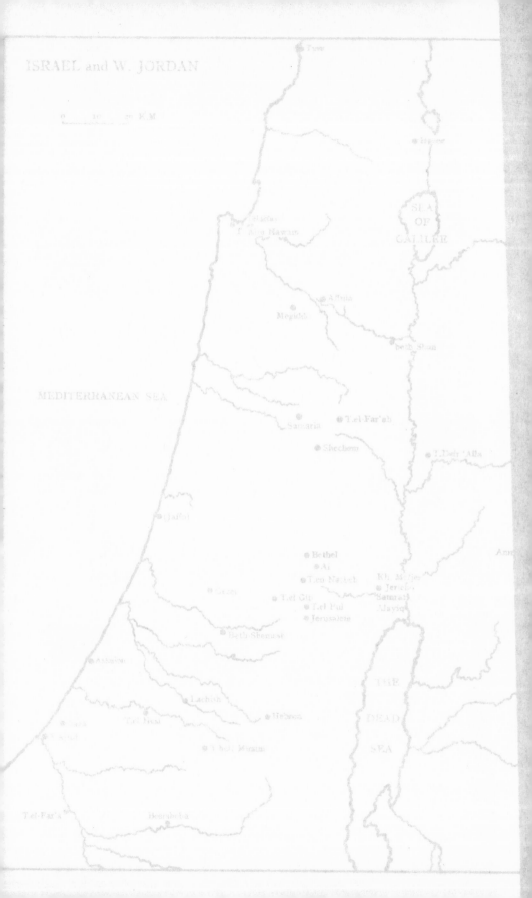

ISRAEL and W. JORDAN

0   10   20 K.M.

Tyre

Hazor

SEA
OF
GALILEE

Chafna
T. Abu Hawam

Afula

Megiddo

Beth Shan

MEDITERRANEAN SEA

Samaria

T. el-Far'ah

Shechem

T. Deir 'Alla

(Jaffa)

Bethel

Amm

Ai

T.en Nasbeh

Kh. M. jar

Gezer

Jericho

T. el Gib

Samari

T. el-Ful

Jayin

Jerusalem

Beth Shemesh

Ashdod

THE

Lachish

DEAD

Gaza

T. el-Hesi

Hebron

SEA

T.en

T. Beit Mirsim

Tel-Far'a

Beersheba